The Story of Travel Air
Makers of Biplanes and Monoplanes

*"The Standard of
Aircraft Comparison"*

by
Travel Air Manufacturing Co.
Wichita, Kansas

©2013 Periscope Film LLC
All Rights Reserved
ISBN#978-1-937684-17-4

Flying—Its Meaning to the World

To cross the continent in 32 hours with sanity and safety; to breakfast in New York and dine in Chicago; to leave Kansas City in the morning and arrive in Los Angeles by nightfall; to sit in ones office at noon and fill a business engagement 600 miles away by evening! These are the realities of today! Aviation—practical aviation, has made them possible by shortening time and space to a minimum.

The spectacular phase of flying has passed. The daredevils of the air have ceased to fly for entertainment and now fly for business. The lessons learned through the part played by aviation during the World War were lessons of proficiency. Trans-continental, trans-oceanic and round-the-world flights by hardy, courageous pioneers have not been made merely to defy nature and her elements but to convincingly demonstrate the entire practicability of *aviation as transportation*.

A step at a time—slowly but none the less surely has come the realization that the day of personal air transportation is here —that aviation is now on a permanent commercial basis.

Since building and delivering its first plane, the Travel Air Company has steadfastly adhered to exacting and proven standards of construction that each ship delivered would adequately serve the interests of commerce and industry in saving time.

The foundation of its success is intensive and constant study; an extraordinary knowledge and experience in aircraft construction; unexcelled manufacturing facilities; unquestioned financial responsibility; and nation wide distribution.

Its record is one of constant progress and achievement. Its president, Walter Beech, won the Ford Reliability Tour in 1926 in a Travel Air Type 4000, a performance and reliability record which still stands.

Thousands upon thousands of flying hours in carrying the air mail and in commercial flying attest Travel Air dependability in all kinds of weather.

The place of Travel Air in the aviation industry is secure, firm, acknowledged. Its ships are in daily use in practically every civilized country. Its name and fame are recognized and applauded the world over. It smiles and grows.

The Yesterday and Today of Transportation

THE era of transportation began centuries ago when the Chieftain of an ancient tribe climbed upon the back of one of his slaves and demanded a ride. Thus long before history began, the inherent desire of mankind for transportation from place to place was crudely satisfied.

As civilization hesitatingly groped forward, the need was felt of getting from place to place more rapidly. Barter and trade was developing business acumen. He who had transportation had the advantage. The broad back of the slave was no longer adequate—too rough riding—too slow. Then came two long poles supporting a wicker basket for a seat with man power at each end—a swinging motion as the occupant rode in more speed and comfort to trade hemp for food and meet in conference on the problems of tribal relations and protection from territorial invasion.

Civilization quickly outgrew man power as a transportation factor—too slow—too wasteful. Why not ride the beast of burden —the cow, the ox, the camel? Lo! it was done and again business was speeded up. Soon the carrying power of the beast was found to be far less than his pulling power —hence the drag—then the cart, the creaking wagon, the one horse shay, the buggy, the coach and the carriage.

Truly the zenith of transportation for business and personal use! But not so. A seething humanity urged ever onward by inrushing competition needed still more adequate means to get from place to place in time—on time. Fulton's steamboat followed the sailing vessel. Iron rails across mountain and plain sent the prairie schooner scurrying to a permanent resting place as a nation was unified by transportation and its commodities distributed from far east to extreme west—north to south.

Had transportation reached its zenith? Far from it. An increasing population needed more elbow room—more and better personal transportation and so first came the one-cylinder automobile—then hard roads—then the modern motor car produced in unbelievable volume to fill the need for speed in personal transportation.

Now at last man has wings. The air age is here. The logical and inevitable has come to pass. The sky is now the battle ground of modern business with no cross roads to impede traffic and with speed, as you will, yet with comfort and safety. Air travel is now a recognized and accepted means of transportation for he who would conserve his time that every hour may be most profitable.

The urge of modern business demanded the airplane. Now that it is here—now that it is economical—now that it is dependable and safe—now that it is comfortable and easy to learn to fly, the question no longer is "Can I afford one, but can I afford to be without one?"

The First Travel Air Built

Old Number One Comes Home to Stay

OLD Travel Air No. 1 has had an interesting career. Bought in 1924 by O. E. Scott, of St. Louis, its first trip was to call on Henry Ford. It was the first new production job Lindbergh ever flew. It has felt the hands of the great and near great at its controls. In it many prominent bankers, financiers and business men have flown. In it Nungesser and Ruth Elder have made more than one trip. And after having been all over the country on various missions it has at last come home to rest with the honor and sentiment that is its due.

This old ship has had 1750 hours in the air with no replacement. It is still airworthy—still trim. It doesn't look out of place among the latest Travel Air ships staked out along the line at the factory.

Following No. 1 have come hundreds of Travel Airs—in seven types, including the new Cabin Monoplane, "The Limousine of the Air"—each filling a commercial need—all characteristic of Travel Air proven performance with dependability.

The history of Travel Air has been a history of aggressiveness and progress from the day its first ship was built. Its ships are the standard of aircraft comparison and merit the full attention of dealers and prospective buyers the world over

One of the Latest Type Travel Airs

The Travel Air Factory of 1926

Travel Air Smiles and Grows

Unknown five years ago—building a plane at a time by hand in a 30x30 foot space in the rear of an old planing mill!

Today ample finance—fifth year of continuous manufacturing to exacting standards—a thoroughly modern five unit factory with over 116,000 feet of floor space, completely equipped in each department; night and day operation to produce, in steadily increasing quantities, 3 types of dual control monoplanes, and 8 types of open cockpit biplanes!

Such is the record of The Travel Air Company—the giant of the airplane industry.

The Travel Air Factory of 1927-1928

The long flying experience and indomitable courage of Walter Beech; the loyalty of a handful of his original associates; the spirit of all employees; a constant adherance to proven principles of safety construction; service with promptness by a nation-wide selling organization! This is the foundation upon which Travel Air has built—the reasons for its steady growth and unquestioned success.

Five unit Travel Air Factory of 1929—116,000 feet of floor space, filled with the most modern machinery

Travel Air administration building, occupied Jan. 1st, 1929

Travel Air field is one of the best and best known flying fields in the country—rich in tradition—and one of the busiest and most carefully regulated in the entire United States.

This field is located on the most accessible air route from the North and East to the Southwest and California, with a lighted airway from Dallas to Kansas City and the East. Seldom does an hour pass in the flying season but that some large or small airplane, from a distance, on business or pleasure, "sets down" upon its firm, fully drained turf—truly a cosmopolitan center—a mecca in a nation in which distances are now annihilated by Aviation, and miles are a matter of seconds in the air.

With comfortable hotels but four miles uptown, on a surfaced road, it is not unusual for San Diego groups to trade experiences with Boston parties at dinner on the second evening of their flight from home.

Should you come to the factory to accept delivery on a "fly away" job, you will enjoy your visit. Guides will direct you and courtesy cars are at your disposal.

Travel Air field is completely and modernly equipped for service and for servicing visiting ships. It is the terminal of the Central Air Lines passenger and flying service. Upon this field all Travel Air planes are thoroughly flight tested before shipment or "fly away."

The flight testing of Travel Air planes is as thorough and exacting as the factory operations and the inspection system. Only by putting each Travel Air plane to the most rigorous test after final assembly can it be fully demonstrated that each workman has done his job the way it should be done and that the plane will deliver performance with dependability to its owner. All flight testing is done by the chief test pilot.

Travel Air field in 1927 upon the occasion of an air meet

With the Camera in the Travel Air Factory

THE first airplanes like the first motor cars were made by hand, one at a time. It was logical and right that this method be followed, for only through painstaking careful hand operations, trial and test, could theoretical factors of construction be proved practical. Not until every detail of construction of the motor car or the airplane was thoroughly demonstrated as commercially practical could jigs, dies and manufacturing standards be established and rigorously maintained.

The history of the Travel Air Company has been no exception to this established and long recognized fact. Its first ship and many succeeding ones were built one at a time, by hand, in the rear of an old planing mill at Wichita. Men who had been flying for years personally worked at the benches to incorporate every phase of their experience into these ships. Other men, masters of their craft, gave unsparingly of their time and skill to improve and perfect even the smallest detail. Still other men who had come to feel the importance of commercial aviation, and who saw the coming demand for a plane built for endurance, safety and performance, were not afraid to stake their money in an endeavor to make a plane to meet the most rigid tests.

The extent to which these earnest, aggresive groups of men have succeeded can be seen from an examination of the photographs of Travel Air's growth as depicted in the preceding section. The new factory of five units, designed for utilizing the most modern production methods, is the largest commercial airplane factory in the world.

Approximately four years ago the Travel Air Company reached the place in its development and progress where it felt justified in entering the commercial airplane field. With this decision made, the company was immediately confronted with the even more important problem of a factory arranged, manned, and equipped for volume production at competitive selling prices yet without sacrifice of quality. Even with the experience of the automobile manufacturer as a general guide, there were no airplane precedents whatsoever to follow, for this was one of the first airplane manufacturers to undertake volume production.

Study and analysis led to the conclusion that six factors enter into the construction of a good commercial airplane. These are: safety, airworthiness, performance, durability, comfort, and appearance. While the relative importance of these qualities varies somewhat with the type of ship, in all cases safety is the paramount issue.

A safe airplane must leave the ground within a reasonably short distance, be able to climb rapidly under good control, have a reliable motor and controls, be structurally substantial, not spin if stalled, and land easily.

Air worthiness embodies stability, steadiness in rough air, and controllability with light or heavy loads.

Performance includes take-off distance and time, rate of climb, ceiling, high speed, landing speed, landing distance, fuel economy, and cruising range.

The other factors of durability, comfort, and appearance need no explanation.

Assuming the analysis just stated to be

fundamentally correct, the important problem remained of planning for production on that basis and then putting the plan into practical operation.

First, consider for a moment the steps involved in producing a new model. They are: (1) design for simplicity of construction and assembly with as many identical fittings and parts as possible, (2) engineering, (3) detail, (4) fabrication, (5) testing. The general design is first worked up in the rough. Then a stress analysis is made of the structure to determine the correct size of the members. Changes in the original design are frequently made at this point to improve conditions which by analysis are shown to be unsatisfactory. The detail drawings are then made and sent to the shop. The production of the first two or three planes is always more or less experimental, but if the engineering is well done, the performance is accurately calculated and is found to vary only slightly from that found by actual tests. From then on the problems of commercial production include materials, factory equipment, labor, and a production schedule.

The materials for construction are chosen, first, for strength, durability, and lightness; second, for ease of manufacture; third, for reliability of supply; and fourth, for price.

In no manufacturing business is the human element more vital than in the building of an airplane. But skilled workmanship can accomplish little with inferior materials. It is perhaps one of the outstanding features of the Travel Air manufacturing system, that all materials are rigidly tested and inspected before they are allowed to enter into the fabrication of Travel Air planes. Tests are made on glue, for instance, to determine the kind which behaves the best under service conditions.

Fuselage welding department—In this large light room all welding operations are conducted by skilled employees who use the most modern welding equipment. Each operation is thoroughly tested before the fuselage moves on for engine mounting.

Monoplane Fuselage being welded on a jig—Welding on a jig locates each tube accurately making all fuselages of the same type identical.

Similarly, cloth, shellac, paint, etc., are tested for quality.

Price is always a secondary consideration. The Travel Air Company believes that a few extra dollars spent on the materials of an airplane to insure its performance and possibly the lives of its occupants is well worth while. Therefore, all structural materials, wood and steel, are thoroughly inspected and tested. A man highly experienced in fine lumbers, personally inspects all spruce, plywood, etc., that enter the wood working department. Each shipment of steel tubing received at the factory is tested for yield point, ultimate strength and elongation.

The engineering department is able to function more efficiently with the aid of these tests. By accurately knowing the strength of steel used in fabrication, the engineer can design parts to a close degree of refinement. This knowledge combined with the use of alloy steels and accurate heat treatment enable Travel Air planes to be designed with uniform strength down to the smallest detail. Fittings which are usually neglected in the structural analysis are designed with the utmost care. The landing gear, which is subjected to such terrific punishment, is exceptionally sturdy. Control surfaces, which can be designed merely for strength, are designed for rigidity as well and are far above the Department of Commerce specifications.

Factory machinery and equipment must be commensurate with production. It requires perhaps less equipment to manufacture an airplane than any product selling at its price. This means that any one with a few tools, an acetylene tank and blow torch, some steel tubing, and an engine on order can start "manufacturing" airplanes. This condition is unfortunate because it permits many people to enter the business who are not adequately equipped in experience and financial backing, and accounts in part for the existence of some 140 or more airplane companies in the United States today.

At the start of any new manufacturing endeavor, labor usually consists of all-round mechanics upon whose ingenuity depends the success of the project. This

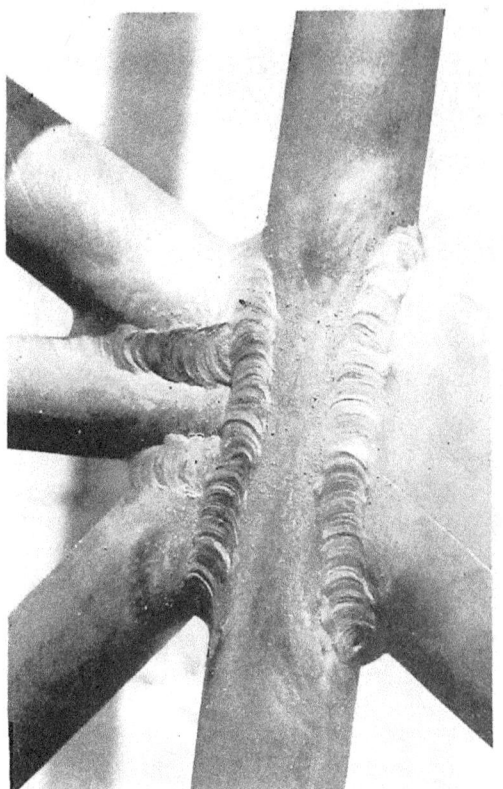 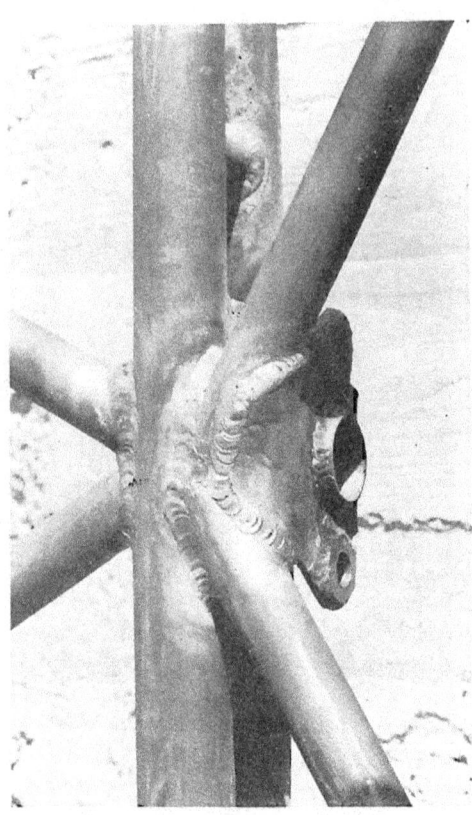

Typical Travel Air Welds—A good weld must be rugged without being heavy or bulky. Just the right amount of metal must be run into the weld. Only the most experienced welders are employed.

applies with special force to the airplane. As the organization grows the labor involved in production becomes more specialized, for specialization is the basis of efficient production. The all-round man is replaced by a craftsman who devotes his time to one particular operation and gains skill and efficiency each day. Often the all-round man develops into the specialized job. Departmentalization of the factory rapidly follows, the old and tried men becoming foremen of the various departments. Personal work comes into being. The welfare of the workmen is found to be for the good of the product as well as the contentment and satisfaction of all employees.

We try, wherever practical, to give our men the "feel of the air" by taking them up. This gives them a feeling of grave responsibility in their work in knowing that the lives of the users of airplanes are largely in their hands in building safety into the airplane.

Travel Air is fortunate in having the resources necessary to build and equip a modern factory that employs a thousand workmen. An idea of this factory and its production methods may be obtained from the following pages.

Travel Airs are designed according to the best proven methods. The fuselage framework is built of seamless steel tubing, faired with wood, and covered with the highest grade of fabric.

The manufacture of Travel Airs naturally divides into two sections, the steel fuselage section and the wood wing section. These form the two principal units of the airplane. It is logical, therefore, that their fabrication should be independent of each other. It is however necessary that their production schedule be co-ordinated to permit wings and fuselage to be com-

Worm Gear Stabilizer Adjusting Mechanism—The entire mechanism is rigid, free from vibration and operates easily.

by efficient experts to suit the particular requirements of Travel Air.

Let us trace the manufacture of a fuselage thru the factory. Steel tubing is cut to the proper lengths on a power saw, designed expressly for aircraft work, and welded up on a jig which locates each tube accurately, making all fuselages of the same type identical. Aircraft welding requires accuracy beyond the limits found in the manufacture of most other welded products. The weld must be rugged without being heavy or bulky. To accomplish this the welder must take particular pains in running just the right amount of metal into the weld. Travel Air insures uniformly good welds by employing highly skilled welders and by careful inspection.

Before the fuselage leaves the jig it is inspected and okayed. It is then lifted from the jig and passes down the assembly line, where fittings, wood superstructure, controls, instruments and equipment are installed. Travel Air fittings for attaching wings, landing gear, engine mounting, etc., have strength without bulk or weight.

The Travel Air stabilizer is easily adjusted while in flight. The adjustment on the cabin monoplanes is operated by a

pleted simultaneously for final assembly.

The complete production system of the new five unit factory has been worked out

Cabin Monoplane Fuselage showing welded steel structure—ready for the wood superstructure.

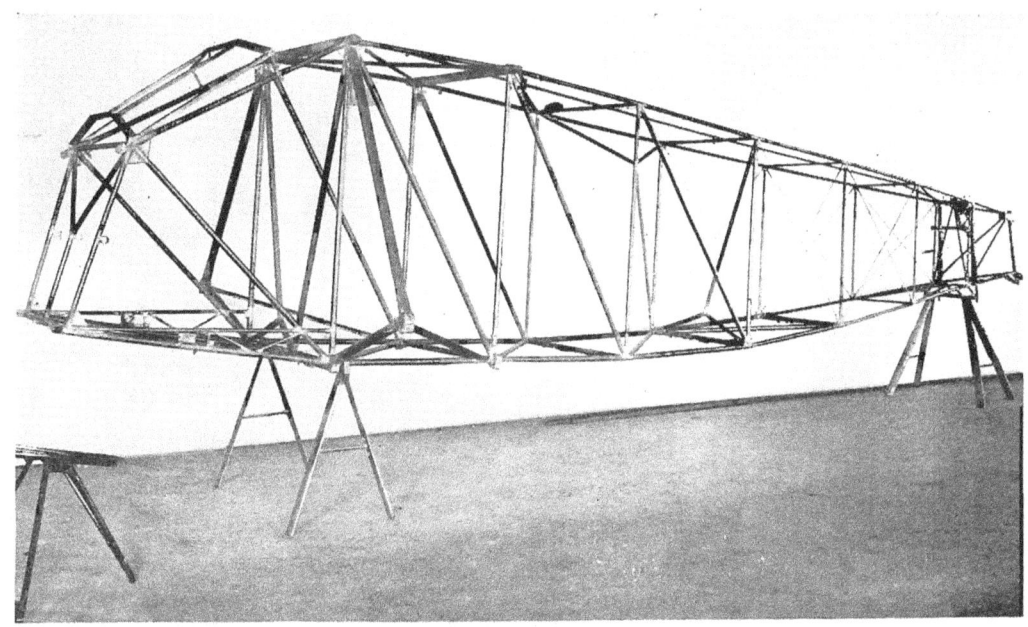

A cabin monoplane on its way through the factory. Wood superstructure is complete. Next comes the fuselage covering and the "dope" room where the airplane cloth is shrunk to drum-like tightness.

A section of the dope and paint room showing monoplanes and wings being doped and polished.

crank mounted at the top of the cabin. A shaft equipped with universal joints and ball bearings and completely enclosed under the upholstery extends back to the worm and sector adjustment at the stabilizer. The entire mechanism is rigid, free from vibration, and operates easily. Other controls work with the minimum of effort making it as easy to fly a Travel Air as to drive an automobile.

Accessibility is one of the features of Travel Air planes. The cowling is easily and quickly removed. Zipper inspection covers are installed to enable ready inspection of control fittings.

Purchasers of Travel Air planes experience a feeling of security in their ships, well-grounded on fact. No commercial airplane in production has as faultless a record of reliability and durability as the Travel Air. The fact that the hidden parts, internal structure, wires, fittings, etc., are made with such extreme care, explains, in part,

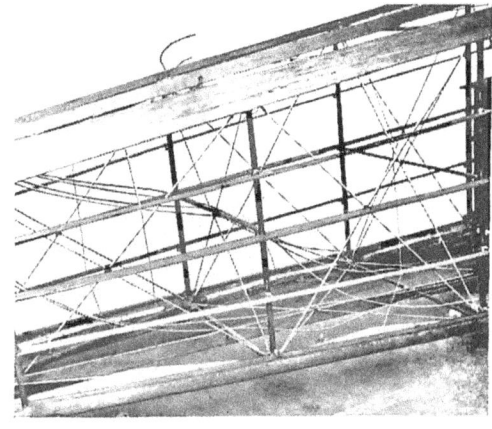

Fuselage with steel wire bracing and wood superstructure being put in place.

the utter freedom of Travel Air from structural failures.

These refinements of detail carried out through the entire ship, together with uniform structural strength and the in-

Another section of the dope and paint room showing wings being sprayed. In this room particular attention is given to ventilation by huge fans.

herent airworthiness of all Travel Air planes have made the enviable reputation which Travel Air enjoys today.

Travel Air jealously guards this reputation and by a policy of constant progress in design and production will always retain its leadership.

Comfort is in no way overlooked in the Travel Air. The days have long passed when passengers or pilot are expected to endure discomfort in the ships they fly, just as the days have gone into history of automobiles without tops, windshields, or spare tires. Travel Air users, whether pilots or passengers, fly with a maximum of physical comfort and convenience, irrespective of the type of Travel Air.

In the Cabin Monoplane — "The Limousine of the Air"—is found every practical comfort yet attainable in aircraft construction. The spacious cabin permits passengers to exchange seats at will with the relief pilot while in flight.

This arrangement is ideal, too, for the owner who is desirous of instruction. In this luxurious cabin, all six occupants face forward seated in upholstered wicker chairs, and with full front and side vision —a distinctive feature.

This cabin is ventilated by the windows of a sedan. Large doors permit ease in entering and leaving the ship. Even in the open types of Travel Air ships comfort of pilot and passengers is not overlooked. Every device and equipment is used to make each and every trip a satisfaction instead of a hardship—a pleasure instead of a task.

The wood super-structure rounds out the fuselage and forms the pleasing lines of the Travel Air body. The steel fuselage framework is completely enclosed by the woodwork making a clean looking interior. The wood super-structure in addition to forming the lines of the plane, adds strength and rigidity to the fuselage.

Before the plane leaves the assembly line it is given a thorough inspection. At this point in its construction all parts are

After engine installation the plane passes to the final assembly department where wings are put on and countless details of assembly are checked.

A section of the completely equipped machine and sheet metal shop.

Nearly ready for the wings—In this department engines are swung in place by an overhead carriage system and chain hoists. Speed with exactness is obtained. In the rear of this room is the completely equipped machine shop.

exposed to the trained eyes of the inspectors. The next step in the manufacture is the covering of the fuselage, then doping, and finally painting.

When the assembled fuselage receives its okay from the inpection department, it passes to the upholstering and covering departments where the highest grade of airplane cloth is stretched tightly over the wood form work, tacked, and sewed. The cloth is then doped. Dope is a nitro-cellulose product that causes a large amount of shrinkage when applied to cloth. The fabric is stretched drum-tight by the time three or four coats have been applied. After the last coat of dope has dried and the surface has been carefully rubbed down, the fuselage is ready for its first shot of lacquer over the surface. As soon as the lacquer dries, it is rubbed down and another coat is sprayed on. This process is repeated until the required finish results.

The cowling struts and various smaller parts are painted separately. Metal parts receive two or three coats of primer before being shot with lacquer.

The fuselage passes from the paint room to the engine installation department. The engines are mounted, gasoline lines, oil lines, and controls are connected. Exhaust manifold and heater installations are made. The complete installation is then checked before the ship passes to the next assembly station where cowling, landing gear, and tail surfaces are assembled.

Travel Air cowling is made accurately by expert sheet metal workers. The cowling is complete around the engine cylinders, exhaust ring, carburetor, etc., giving the ship a finished appearance. When engine, landing gear, tail surfaces, and cowling are installed the ship is complete with the exception of the wings and struts.

The plane is sent thru the paint room

In the wood working department the spars and other wood members assume shape. Here also the wings are fashioned. Though later concealed by fabric, the interior structure must consist of a large number of precise operations to insure adequate strength and light weight.

ABOVE—

  Monoplane wing structure—Monoplane spars are built of laminated wood. By careful design, and selection of perfect material the greatest strength for a given weight is obtained by the laminated process.

BELOW—

  2000 Ton gluing press used in making biplane spars.

Wing spar in first stages of construction———One of the first operations in making up the finished spar, a cross section of which is shown below.

once more for a final finishing and polishing and then enters the final assembly and rigging department. The wing is dropped into place, struts and wires are rigged, and the ship is given a final inspection before being test flown.

It is necessary that the wings should be ready for assembling at this point. A rigid manufacturing schedule permits the simultaneous completion of wings and fuselage and the uninterrupted production of completed ships. By adhering closely to the most advanced theories of straight line production, parts scheduling, and stock control Travel Air is able to cut factory costs to a minimum.

The price that is paid for a Travel Air ship goes for *quality* and not excess overhead, muddled production, and surplus stock.

The wings form the other important unit of the airplane. These are manufactured in a separate building adjoining the paint and dope department. Let us now trace their manufacture.

WINGS—The lumber storage is located at the extreme end of the wing factory. All wood is drawn from this stock and is carefully inspected by an expert before going to the mill room to be cut to the proper size and shape. The well-equipped mill room furnished with the most modern machinery presents an interesting contrast to the hand made, cut and try methods of only a few years ago. The use of jigs for cutting and drilling as well as assembling permits a large production from a few workers. But more important it means accuracy—accuracy in wood working which was not thought of a few years ago. Each part when assembled fits smoothly and closely into its position making a strong but light structure.

Laminated spars are not inclined to warp. Note how the grain of the two wood sections are arranged so that one offsets the shrink or swelling of the other.

Travel Air wings are of proven design. The two spars form the backbone of the wing. Upon their strength depend the lives of the occupants of the airplane. It is, therefore, with the utmost care that the spars are designed and fabricated. The two spars are held in place by the compression ribs and drag trussing. The shape of the ribs form the wing curve. Therefore, they serve two purposes as structural members, and as shape-forming members. The ribs are not merely slipped on the spar and allowed to float loosely as in some designs, but are fastened rigidly in place. At the leading and trailing edges they are tied together by means of a light strip of duralumin.

Biplane spars are built in two halves, glued and pressed together. Monoplane spars are built up of laminated wood. By careful design and selection of perfect material the greatest strength for a given weight is obtained by the laminated process.

Material that has been milled passes to the wing assembly department and is assembled in jigs. Ribs are built up first in separate jigs and are then assembled on the

Rib being assembled on spars—a delicate and exacting assembly.

spars. After the ribs are assembled, the wing gasoline tanks are installed. The tanks are held rigidly in place and are mounted on felt to prevent vibration. The section of the wing at the tank is covered with plywood to give additional rigidity.

Travel Air produced the first successful retractable landing light. It costs more, but by entirely disappearing into the wing, offers no resistance when not in use. The landing lights are worm driven by a crank located within easy reach of the pilot, and operate smoothly in all positions. All Travel Air monoplanes may be equipped with this type of landing light.

The ailerons are of the inset hinge type, (commonly called Frieze). By placing the hinge point inside the aileron an aerodynamical balance is produced as the aileron is moved thru its entire range, giving easy and smooth operation. When the aileron is in the neutral position, it conforms exactly to the wing curve presenting no additional drag.

When completely assembled the wing is inspected carefully by an expert. Any defect no matter how slight gets a yellow ticket which means reject. If the wing is found to be perfect it receives a green O. K. ticket and is covered. It is then taken to the dope room and given seven coats of dope before it passes to the paint room. After the wing is sprayed with lacquer and polished, it is ready to be rigged on the fuselage in the final assembly department.

The control surfaces of new designs are

Wing tank assembly in wing. A splendid example of clean cut, exact, painstaking work.

all sand load tested as well as being calculated for strength. The sand load test is entirely practical for it simulates the actual conditions when the airplane is in flight. The sand is accurately weighed in one, five and ten pound sacks. The surfaces are rigged on the airplane and a weight of sand corresponding to an air load, greater than any that could be imposed in a manoeuvre, is distributed on the surface. If the surface stands up under the load without much deflection, it is considered satisfactory.

The Travel Air inspection system is operated by a department formed expressly for that purpose. Hit and miss inspection by department foremen is done away with and in its place a rigid and efficient inspection system is in force. An inspector is located in each department who reports directly to the chief inspector. Each part is therefore, inspected at its point of manufacture, and the whole assembly is inspected at various stages of production.

Monoplane wing showing aileron control and compartment for retractable landing lights. Travel Air produced the first successful retractable landing light.

Monoplane wing tip showing method of attachment of Frieze type ailerons.

Sand load testing of new designs are an outstanding safety factor in Travel Air construction.

A close-up view of the drag rods and compression rib—showing precision in manufacturing and assembly.

In the wood working room is installed complete wood working machinery of the most modern kind. Each piece of wood used is clear, straight grained with no knots or blemishes, and is sawed and planed to most exacting requirements.

Biplane wings being covered. After the covering is stretched over the wings and stitched in position it is given seven coats of cellulose nitrate which shrinks the covering drum tight.

One of the many inspections every Travel Air plane is given.

No units or assemblies are permitted on the airplane without the official green ticket of the inspection department.

Finally the completed airplane is checked in every detail, test flown, and rechecked, before it is given the approval for bearing the name Travel Air thru the skies.

* * * * * *

A cordial invitation to personally visit the enlarged Travel Air factory is extended to all of the air-minded, whether or not they be prospective purchasers.

A revelation in the progress of airplane construction awaits the eyes of any visitor. Here will be found the latest and best machinery that can be purchased for the making of airplanes. The most modern manufacturing practices will be found in vogue. Line assembly is maintained. Anyone so inclined may start in the fuselage welding department and follow a certain airplane through each department to final assembly and then fly in it a few days later.

Trained guides cheerfully accompany visitors through all departments, explaining all details of fabrication and manufacture. We are never more pleased than when dealers and friends come and see for themselves. Any visitor will leave the factory with a bigger and better idea of the magnitude and steadily increasing growth of this newest of all industries—Aviation.

In addition to the factory itself, the visitor will see the days production staked out on the line and in addition see one of the best airports in the country with ships almost constantly in the air.

The Travel Air factory is located on its own airport, some four miles directly east of Wichita, on surfaced roads from downtown. Buses pass the door on half hour schedules.

Travel Air—
The Plane of Performance

TRAVEL AIR'S claim to superiority is based on the fact that it has never attempted the freakish, or the untried, nor employed any method or material by which low cost might be achieved at the sacrifice of safety or dependability.

Thus it is that Travel Air has built three types of Cabin Monoplanes and nine types of open cockpit biplanes that have taken the foremost place in commercial aviation—a plane for every need—training, sport, light transport and personal business use. Travel Air holds its enviable place in the aviation world not alone by its ability to always take the air on an instant's notice; not alone by its ability to conquer the climatic conditions of high and low altitudes with the same reliability; not alone by its ability to render efficient service in the face of high or low winds—not alone by its inherent stability and ease of control—but upon a combination of all of these accomplishments.

The Travel Air record of air worthiness that started with old Number One, has been maintained in every ship of every type that has since left the factory.

In the On-to-Sesqui race from California to Philadelphia, the Travel Air entry crossed the Rockies on the Continental Air Mail course with the greatest of ease and sureness, finishing in first place. Two months later, the same type of plane, flying from Los Angeles to Boston over the same route, encountered a 100 mile gale, going through rain and lightning without a mishap. It crossed the high elevation of the Rockies with the same sureness that it showed in cruising the extremely low levels of the Salton Sea.

In the 1928 New York to Los Angeles Class A race, a privately owned Travel Air biplane, encountering all kinds of weather in high and low altitude, was never late at a "control," and flew steadily and surely across the American Continent to win, over all biplanes that were entered in this grueling contest of speed and endurance.

Skilled air men are attracted to Travel Air by its economy of operation and the absence of replacement expense and attention. The record of Travel Air Plane No. 1 in flying 1750 hours, in every kind of weather, and under all kinds of circumstances without replacement expense is being repeated daily by Travel Air Planes.

Travel Air reliability in service is another factor that gains for it a foremost place. In the winning of first place in the 1926 Ford Reliability Tour, where load, speed, engine displacement, flying time, and stick time and unstick time is entered into consideration, Travel Air came through with the greatest number of points, a record never duplicated.

In the mail and passenger service, where lifting power plus the ability to maintain a definite schedule are deciding factors, Travel Air has taken a definite place—and is meeting these rigid requirements, with the result that the 6 Place Cabin Monoplane is fast becoming the accepted light transport passenger carrying ship.

In trans-oceanic flights, Travel Air has proved its dependability. The "Woolaroc," piloted by Art Goebel, built from standard Travel Air specifications, came up to the most exacting tests in finishing first over 1700 miles of ocean between San Francisco and Honolulu.

Travel Air owes its enviable place in commercial aviation to a combination of steadiness, reliability, and safety in every day service—the performances of major importance—and it is in this accomplishment that Travel Air takes the greatest pride, realizing that the expansion of air travel depends not on individual accomplishment, but on proved stability in regular service.

The Travel Air Fleet

Consists of

3 Dual Control Cabin Monoplanes

and

9 Open Cockpit, 3-place Biplanes

A Plane for Every Commercial Need—Training, Sport, Personal Business or Light Transport

The Travel Air Six-place Cabin Monoplane Type A-6000-A
With Wasp 420 H. P. Engine

SPECIFICATIONS

CAPACITY—
  *2 pilots, 4 passengers @ 170 lbs. and 110 lbs. baggage, or equivalent.

PERFORMANCE WITH NORMAL FULL LOAD—
  Landing speed..60 M. P. H.
  High speed (sea level)..............................138 M. P. H.
  Rate of climb (sea level).........................1000 ft. per min.
  Take-off time (full load, no wind at sea level) 14 sec.
  Take-off in feet..500 ft.
  Landing run (without use of brakes)............700 ft.
  Climb to 5,000 ft..6 min.
  Climb to 10,000 ft.......................................15 min.
  Climb to 15,000 ft.......................................29 min.

  Service ceiling..18,000 ft.
  Absolute ceiling..20,000 ft.
  Cruising speed at 1620 R. P. M..................110 M. P. H.
  Cruising speed at 1800 R. P. M..................120 M. P. H.
  Cruising range at 1620 R. P. M. (21 gal. per hr. equals 6.25 hours or 650-700 miles.)

DIMENSIONS—
  Span...54 ft. 5 in.
  Over-all length...31 ft. 1½ in.
  Over-all height..9 ft. ½ in.
  Total Wing area...340 sq. ft.

POWER PLANT—Wasp 420 H. P. Engine.

*NOTE—We are now working with the Department of Commerce to get the Wasp approved so that we can carry a differential load of gas which will enable us to carry 7 passengers and pilot on short hops.
  This data is not complete at this printing. However, we expect to have it approved in a short time.

SPECIFICATIONS [Continued]

WEIGHTS—
  Weight empty . . . . 3290 lbs.
  Useful load . . . . 1960 lbs.
  Pay load . . . . 930 lbs.
  Weight fully loaded . . . . 5250 lbs.

Weight empty includes, cabin insulation (for heat and sound), large luggage compartment to rear of cabin, pressure fire extinguisher, cabin exhaust heaters, complete night flying equipment (2 landing lights, Navigation lights, instrument board lights, cabin light, 70 Amp-hour storage battery, 2 parachute flares), generator (engine driven) and regulator, combination hand electric inertia engine starter, ventilated cowling, metal propeller, 36x8 wheels, dual controls, complete set flying electrical and engine instruments, six upholstered seats for passengers and pilots, tail wheel, first aid kit.

  Pay load including 5 passengers @ 170 lbs. . . . . 850 lbs.
    and 80 lbs. of baggage, total . . . . 930 lbs.
  Useful load includes pay load @ 930 lbs., 1 pilot @ 170 lbs.; 10 gallons oil @ 8 lbs. equals 80 lbs.; 130 gallons fuel @ 6 lbs. equals 780 lbs., total—1960 lbs.

EQUIPMENT [and other particulars]

COLOR—Standard production color, black fuselage with orange fuselage stripe and orange wings, or in green and orange or blue and orange.

INTERIOR FINISH—

Upholstery—Standard—Blue or taupe Chase Velmo Cut Mohair or fine quality of broadcloth.
  Special quality of broadcloth or mohair $200.00 additional.

CABIN FURNISHING—

Chairs—Six steel frame removable wicker chairs upholstered to harmonize with cabin interior.
  Rest Room in rear of cabin $195.00 additional.

Windows—Plate glass raised and lowered by auto type crank lifts. Shatter proof glass in front of pilots compartment.

WHEELS—32x6 equipped with 36x8 tires.

BRAKES—Bendix.

HEATERS—Located on each side of front of cabin.

LIGHTS—Instrument lights, navigation lights.

NIGHT FLYING EQUIPMENT—Complete with landing lights, 12 volt battery and two flares—$500.00 additional.

LETTERING—"TRAVEL AIR" on fin and nose of fuselage.

CONTROLS—Dual "dep" side by side.
  Rudder pedals.
  Separately controlled brake pedals.

INSTRUMENTS—
  Tachometer   Air speed indicator
  Oil pressure gauge   Bank and turn indicator
  Oil temperature gauge   Switch, primer
  Magnetic compass   Altimeter
             Clock

FUEL CAPACITY—130 gallon tank in wing roots.
  Fuel, gravity feed.
  Oil capacity, 8 gallons.

GENERAL

Cabin insulation is very effective in insulating against heat and cold. Heaters can be regulated to maintain constant cabin temperatures. Flights have been made to a height of 15,500 ft. above sea level in which the outside temperature registered 35°F. below zero while the cabin temperature was perfectly comfortable without wraps, 60-65°F. Insulation is very effective in deadening sound and conversation can be engaged in normal tone of voice.

This airplane is stable, latterally, directionally and longitudinally and is easy to land.

Three-quarter front view

Travel Air Six-place Monoplane
Type 6000-B

Close-up of Tail Wheel used on Monoplanes.

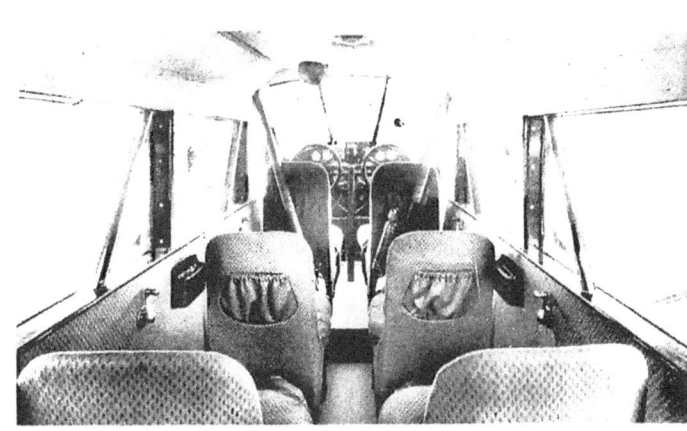

The Travel Air Six-place Cabin Monoplane
Type 6000-B
With J-6 Whirlwind Nine Engine—300 H. P.

SPECIFICATIONS

CAPACITY—
  2 pilots, 4 passengers, and 150 lbs. baggage, or equivalent.

PERFORMANCE WITH NORMAL FULL LOAD—
  High speed at sea level .... 130 M. P. H
  Rate of climb at sea level .... 800 ft. P. M.
  Take-off time, no wind, sea level .... 12 Seconds
  Take-off in feet .... 500 ft.
  Landing run—no brakes .... 700 ft.
  Climb to 5,000 ft. .... 8 min.
  Climb to 10,000 ft. .... 19 min.
  Service ceiling .... 16,000 ft.
  Absolute ceiling .... 18,000 ft.
  Cruising speed .... 110 M. P. H.
  Landing speed .... 60 M. P. H.

DIMENSIONS—
  Over-all span .... 48 ft. 6½ in.
  Height .... 9 ft. 0½ in.
  Over-all length .... 31 ft. 2 in.
  Wing chord .... 78 in.
  Wing area .... 282 sq. ft.

POWER PLANT—
  J-6 Whirlwind Nine Engine-300 H. P.

WEIGHTS—
  Gross weight .... 4230 lbs.
  Weight empty (fully equipped) .... 2700 lbs.
  Pay load, with night flying equipment .... 815 lbs.
  Useful load .... 1530 lbs.

EQUIPMENT [and other particulars]

COLOR—Black fuselage with orange fuselage stripe and orange wings, or green and orange, or blue and orange.

INTERIOR FINISH—High grade broadcloth.

CABIN FURNISHINGS — 6 steel frame removable wicker chairs upholstered to harmonize with cabin interior. Windows plate glass, raised and lowered by auto type crank lifts.

WHEELS—32x6 with 36x8 tires.
  Brakes—Bendix.
  Heaters located on both sides of front of cabin.
  Rest Room—$195 extra.

LETTERING—"Travel Air" on fin. Department of Commerce numbers on wings and rudder.

LIGHTS—Instrument lights, navigation lights.

NIGHT FLYING EQUIPMENT—Complete with landing lights, 12 V. Battery and two flares, $500.00 additional.

CONTROLS—Dual "dep" side by side.
  Rudder pedals.
  Separately controlled brake pedals.

INSTRUMENTS —
  Tachometer   Air speed indicator
  Oil pressure gauge   Bank and turn indicator
  Oil temperature gauge   Switch, primer
  Magnetic compass   Altimeter
            Clock

FUEL CAPACITY—82 gallon tank in wing roots.
  Fuel, gravity feed.
  Oil capacity, 7 gallons.

Three-quarter front view

Travel Air Four-place Monoplane
Type 10-B

Three-quarter rear view

The Travel Air Four-place Cabin Monoplane Type 10-B
With J-6 Whirlwind Nine Engine—300 H. P.

SPECIFICATIONS

CAPACITY—
  Pilot and three passengers.

PERFORMANCE WITH NORMAL FULL LOAD—
  High speed at sea level .... 140 M. P. H.
  Landing speed at sea level .... 55 M. P. H.
  Rate of climb, at sea level .... 1140 ft. per min.
  Take-off time, no wind, sea level .... 11 sec.
  Take-off in feet .... 500 ft.
  Landing run (no brakes) .... 700 ft.
  Climb to 5,000 ft. .... 6 min.
  Climb to 10,000 ft. .... 16 min.
  Service ceiling .... 17,000 ft.
  Absolute Ceiling .... 19,000 ft.
  Cruising speed .... 115 M. P. H.

DIMENSIONS—
  Over-all span (tip to tip) .... 43 ft. 6 in.
  Over-all height .... 8 ft. 8 in.
  Over-all length .... 27 ft. 4½ in.
  Wing chord (upper) .... 74 in.
  Wing area .... 239 sq. ft.

POWER PLANT—
  J-6 Whirlwind Nine-300 H. P.
  Steel propeller

WEIGHTS—
  Gross weight, fully loaded .... 3400 lbs.
  Weight, empty .... 2255 lbs.
  Pay load .... 510 lbs.
  Useful load (2 passengers, pilot, baggage,
    fuel, oil) .... 1145 lbs.

NOTE—This Travel Air Monoplane will also be offered with J-6—Whirlwind Seven—225 H. P. engine as soon as engines of that H. P. are available.

EQUIPMENT [and other particulars]

EQUIPMENT—

COLOR—Black fuselage with orange fuselage stripe and orange wings or green and orange or blue and orange.

INTERIOR FINISH—High grade Broadcloth.

CABIN FURNISHING—4 removable wicker chairs upholstered to harmonize with cabin interior.
  Windows plate glass, raised and lowered by auto type cranklifts.

WHEELS—30x5 with 32x6 tires.
  Brakes—Bendix.
  Heater.

LETTERING—"Travel Air" on fin. Department of Commerce numbers on wings and rudder.

LIGHTS—Instrument lights, navigation lights.

CONTROLS—Dual "dep" side by side.
  Rudder pedals.
  Separately controlled brake pedals.

INSTRUMENTS—
  Tachometer   Oil pressure gauge
  Starter (Series No. 16 Inertia)   Oil temperature gauge
  Magnetic compass   Switch, primer
  Air speed indicator   Altimeter

FUEL CAPACITY—
  70 gallon tank in wing roots.
  Fuel, gravity feed.
  Oil capacity, 8 gallons.

Three-quarter front view

Travel Air Three-place Biplane
Type B9-4000

Three-quarter rear view

Climbability

The Travel Air Three-place Biplane
Type B9-4000
With J-6 Whirlwind Nine—300 H. P. Engine

SPECIFICATIONS

CAPACITY—
  Pilot and two passengers.

PERFORMANCE WITH NORMAL FULL LOAD—
  High speed at sea level .... 135 M. P. H.
  Landing speed .... 50 M. P. H.
  Rate of climb, sea level .... 1500 ft. per min.
  Take-off time, no wind, sea level .... 7 sec.
  Take-off in feet .... 275 ft.
  Landing run (no brakes) .... 400 ft.
  Climb to 5,000 ft .... 4 min.
  Climb to 10,000 ft .... 11 min.
  Service ceiling .... 18,000 ft.
  Absolute ceiling .... 20,000 ft.
  Cruising speed .... 115 M. P. H.

DIMENSIONS—
  Over-all span (tip to tip) .... 33 ft. 0 in.
  Over-all height .... 8 ft. 9 in.
  Over-all length .... 23 ft. 2½ in.
  Wing chord (upper) .... 66 in.
  Wing chord (lower) .... 56 in.
  Wing area .... 289 sq. ft.
  Wing section .... Travel Air No. 1

POWER PLANT—
  J-6 Whirlwind Nine-300 H. P.
  Steel propeller.

WEIGHTS—
  Gross weight, fully loaded .... 2800 lbs.
  Weight, empty .... 1885 lbs.
  Pay load .... 340 lbs.
  Useful load (2 passengers, pilot, baggage,
    fuel, oil) .... 915 lbs.

EQUIPMENT [and other particulars]

COLOR—Fuselage
    Tail Surfaces
    Chassis } Travel Air Blue
    Struts
  Wings—Orange, or color scheme by arrangement.

UPHOLSTERING—Brown Spanish Leather.

LETTERING—"Travel Air" on fin. Department of Commerce numbers on wings and rudder.

WHEELS—30x5 tires.
  Brakes—Bendix.

INSTRUMENTS—
  Tachometer   Altimeter
  Oil pressure gauge   Ignition switch
  Starting magneto   Air speed compass
  Compass   Oil temperature gauge

LIGHTS—Wired for navigation lights. No lights fitted.

CONTROLS—Single, in rear cockpit. (Dual control, $75.00 extra.)

GAS CAPACITY—60 gallons.

FUEL SUPPLY SYSTEM—Gravity.

PASSENGERS—Two in front cockpit. Pilot in rear cockpit.

CHASSIS—Oleo.

STARTER—(Series No. 16 Eclipse.)

Three-quarter front view

Travel Air Three-place Biplane
Type B-4000

Oleo Landing Gear on Biplane

Side view

The Travel Air Three-place Biplane
Type B-4000
With J-5-C Whirlwind Engine—200 H. P.

SPECIFICATIONS

CAPACITY—
  Pilot and two passengers.

PERFORMANCE WITH NORMAL FULL LOAD—
  High speed at sea level..................................125 M. P. H.
  Rate of climb at sea level.........................900 ft. per min.
  Take off 300 ft...8 sec.
  Service ceiling (climb of 100 ft. per min.)....14,000 ft.
  Absolute ceiling..15,500 ft.
  Landing speed...50 M. P. H.
  Normal cruising range (with 68 gal. fuel)....500 to 550 miles

DIMENSIONS—
  Over-all span (tip to tip).............................34 ft. 8 in.
  Over-all height..8 ft. 9 in.
  Over-all length..23 ft. 7 in.
  Wing chord (lower)....................................56 in.
  Wing chord (upper)...................................66 in.

  Wing area...289 sq. ft.
  Wing section..Travel Air No. 1.
  Wing loading..10.1 lbs. per sq. ft.
  Power loading..14.5 lbs. per H. P.

POWER PLANT—
  J-5-C Whirlwind Nine.
  200 H. P. at 1800 R. P. M.
  Fuel consumption at cruising speed
    (1550 R. P. M.)..12 gal. per hr.
  Eclipse hand starter.
  Intake heater.
  Steel propeller standard equipment.

WEIGHTS—
  Gross weight, fully loaded........................2900 lbs.
  Weight, empty..1885 lbs.

EQUIPMENT [and other particulars]

COLOR—Fuselage ⎫
  Tail Surfaces ⎬ Travel Air Blue
  Chassis ⎪
  Struts ⎭
  Wings—Orange

UPHOLSTERING—Brown Spanish Leather.

LETTERING—"Travel Air" on fin. Department of Commerce numbers on wings and rudder.

WHEELS—Wire. 30x5 tires.
  Brakes—Bendix.

INSTRUMENTS—
  Tachometer   Air speed indicator
  Oil pressure gauge   Switch
  Oil temperature gauge   Primer
  Magnetic compass   Altimeter

NIGHT FLYING EQUIPMENT—Complete with landing lights, 12 volt battery and two flares, $500 additional.

LIGHTS—Wings wired for navigation lights. No lights fitted.

CONTROLS—Single stick in rear cockpit.

GAS CAPACITY—68 gallons.

TANK LOCATION—26 gal. in center section. 42 gal. in wing tanks.

GAS SUPPLY SYSTEM—Gravity.

OIL CAPACITY—6 gallons.

OIL TANK LOCATION—In front of fuselage below motor.

PASSENGERS—Two in front cockpit. Pilot in rear cockpit.

CHASSIS—Oleo.

Three-quarter front view

Travel Air Three-place Biplane
Type C-4000

Type "B" Wings—Oleo Landing Gear

Three-quarter rear view

Side view

The Travel Air Three-place Biplane Type C-4000
With Challenger Engine—170 H. P.

SPECIFICATIONS

CAPACITY—
  Pilot and two passengers.

PERFORMANCE WITH NORMAL FULL LOAD—
  High speed at sea level.... 125 M. P. H.
  Rate of climb at sea level... 800 ft. per min.
  Service ceiling (climb of 100 ft. per min.) 14,000 ft.
  Landing speed.. 45 M. P. H.
  Normal cruising range (with 60 gal. fuel) 550-600 miles

DIMENSIONS—
  Over-all span (tip to tip)...... 34 ft. 8 in.
  Over-all height................ 8 ft. 9 in.
  Over-all length................ 24 ft. 6 in.
  Wing chord (lower)............. 56 in.
  Wing chord (upper)............. 66 in.

Wing area .. 296 sq. ft.
Wing section. Travel Air No. 1
Wing loading. 8.8 lb. per sq. ft.
Power loading 15.3 lb. per H. P.

POWER PLANT—
  Challenger 170 H. P. at 1800 R. P. M. Fuel consumption at cruising speed (1550 R. P. M.) 10 gal. per hr. Bosch Booster. Wood propeller standard equipment. (Standard Steel propeller $235 extra.)

WEIGHTS—
  Gross weight, fully loaded . 2600 lbs.
  Weight, empty . 1600 lbs.

EQUIPMENT [and other particulars]

COLOR—Fuselage ⎫
         Tail Surfaces ⎬ Travel Air Blue
         Chassis ⎪
         Struts ⎭
         Wings—Orange.
Or color scheme by arrangement.

UPHOLSTERING—Brown Spanish Leather.

LETTERING—"Travel Air" on fin. Department of Commerce numbers on wings and rudder.

WHEELS—and Tires 28x4.

INSTRUMENTS ·
  Tachometer   Altimeter
  Oil pressure gauge   Ignition switch
          Starting magneto
LIGHTS—Wired for navigation lights. No lights fitted.
CONTROLS—Single, in rear cockpit. (Dual control $75.00 extra.)
GAS CAPACITY—60 gallons.
FUEL SUPPLY SYSTEM—Gravity.
PASSENGERS—Two in front cockpit. Pilot in rear cockpit.
CHASSIS—Rubber shock cord in tension.
HEADREST—Standard.

Three-quarter front view

Travel Air Three-place Biplane
Type E-4000

Three-quarter rear view

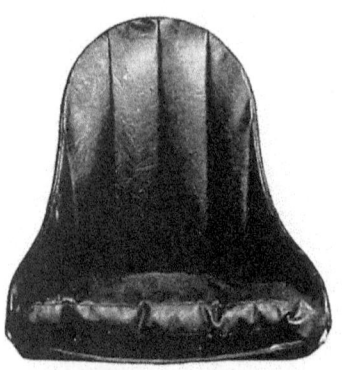

Comfortable seat for pilot in Travel Air Biplanes

The Travel Air Three-place Biplane
Type E-4000
With J-6 Whirlwind Five Engine—165 H. P.

SPECIFICATIONS

At the time this catalog went to press the performance data of this Travel Air biplane had not been taken, due primarily to an increased engine rating from 150 to 165 H. P. Performance data will be ready shortly and supplied on request. The performance, however, will exceed that of the Travel Air biplane with Axelson engine.

EQUIPMENT (and other particulars)

COLOR—Fuselage
    Tail Surfaces
    Chassis } Travel Air Blue.
    Struts
    Wings—Orange, or color scheme by arrangement.
UPHOLSTERING—Brown Spanish Leather.
LETTERING—"Travel Air" on fin. Department of Commerce numbers on wings and rudder.
WHEELS—and tires 28x4.
INSTRUMENTS—
    Tachometer   Altimeter
    Oil pressure gauge   Ignition switch
        Starting magneto

LIGHTS—Wired for navigation lights. No lights fitted.
CONTROLS—Single, in rear cockpit. (Dual control, $75.00 extra.)
GAS CAPACITY—60 gallons.
FUEL SUPPLY SYSTEM—Gravity.
PASSENGERS—Two in front cockpit. Pilot in rear cockpit.
CHASSIS—Rubber shock cord in tension.
HEADREST—Standard.

Three-quarter front view

Travel Air Three-place Biplane
Type W-4000

Three-quarter rear view

Side view

The Travel Air Three-place Biplane
Type W-4000
With Warner-Scarab Engine—110 H. P.

SPECIFICATIONS

CAPACITY—
  Pilot and two passengers.

PERFORMANCE WITH NORMAL FULL LOAD—
  High speed at sea level ....105 M. P. H.
  Landing speed ....43 M. P. H.
  Normal cruising range (with 42 gal. fuel)...400 to 420 miles.

DIMENSIONS—
  Over-all span (tip to tip).............34 ft. 8 in.
  Over-all height...........................8 ft. 9 in.
  Over-all length..........................24 ft. 7 in.
  Wing chord (upper).....................66 in.
  Wing chord (lower).....................56 in.
  Wing area.................................296 sq. ft.
  Wing section.............................Travel Air No. 1

POWER PLANT—
  Warner-Scarab.
  110 H. P. at 1800 R. P. M.
  Fuel consumption at cruising speed .... 8 gal. per hr.
  Wood propeller—stock.
  Adjustable metal propeller, $235.00 extra.

WEIGHTS—
  Gross weight, fully loaded ....2300 lbs.
  Weight, empty..............................1400 lbs.
  Pay load......................................440 lbs.
  Useful load (2 passengers, pilot, baggage, fuel, oil) ....900 lbs.

EQUIPMENT [and other particulars]

COLOR—Fuselage
     Tail Surfaces } Travel Air Blue
     Chassis
     Struts
  Wings—Orange, or color scheme by arrangement.

UPHOLSTERING—Brown Spanish Leather.

LETTERING—"Travel Air" on fin. Department of Commerce numbers on wings and rudder.

WHEELS—and tires 28x4

INSTRUMENTS—
  Tachometer   Altimeter
  Oil pressure gauge   Ignition switch
         Starting magneto

LIGHTS—Wired for navigation lights. No lights fitted.

CONTROLS—Single, in rear cockpit. (Dual control, $75.00 extra.)

GAS CAPACITY—42 gallons.

FUEL SUPPLY SYSTEM—Gravity.

PASSENGERS—Two in front cockpit. Pilot in rear cockpit.

CHASSIS—Rubber shock cord in tension.

Three-quarter front view

Travel Air Three-place Biplane
Type A-4000

Three-quarter rear view

Side view

The Travel Air Three-place Biplane Type A-4000 With Axelson Engine—150 H. P.

SPECIFICATIONS

CAPACITY—
  Pilot and two passengers.

PERFORMANCE WITH NORMAL FULL LOAD—
  High speed at sea level..................110 M. P. H.
  Cruising speed at 1750 R. P. M..........95 M. P. H.
  Rate of Climb..........................525 ft. per min.
  Landing speed..........................45 M. P. H.
  Normal cruising range (with 42 gal. fuel)....400 to 420 miles.

DIMENSIONS—
  Over-all span (tip to tip)..............34 ft. 8 in.
  Over-all height........................8 ft. 9 in.
  Over-all length........................24 ft. 8 in.
  Wing chord (upper).....................66 in.
  Wing chord (lower).....................56 in.

Wing area..............................296 sq. ft.
Wing section...........................Travel Air No. 1

POWER PLANT—
  Axelson
  150 H. P. at 1800 R. P. M.
  Fuel consumption at cruising speed........8 gal. per hr.
  Wood propeller—stock.
  Adjustable metal propeller, $235.00 extra.

WEIGHTS—
  Gross weight, fully loaded..............2600 lbs.
  Weight, empty..........................1600 lbs.
  Pay load...............................425 lbs.
  Useful load (2 passengers, pilot, baggage, fuel, oil)....1000 lbs.

EQUIPMENT [and other particulars]

COLOR—Fuselage
    Tail Surfaces
    Chassis } Travel Air Blue
    Struts
    Wings—Orange, or color scheme by arrangement.

UPHOLSTERING—Leatherwove.

LETTERING—"Travel Air" on fin. Department of Commerce numbers on wings and rudder.

WHEELS—and tires 28x4.

INSTRUMENTS—
  Tachometer   Altimeter
  Oil pressure gauge   Ignition switch
           Starting magneto

LIGHTS—Wired for navigation lights. No lights fitted.

CONTROLS—Single, in rear cockpit. (Dual control, $75.00 extra.)

GAS CAPACITY—60 gallons.

FUEL SUPPLY SYSTEM—Gravity.

PASSENGERS—Two in front cockpit. Pilot in rear cockpit.

CHASSIS—Rubber shock cord in tension.

HEADREST—Standard.

Three-quarter front view

Travel Air Three-place Biplane
Type K-4000

Three-quarter rear view

Side view

44

The Travel Air Three-place Biplane
Type K-4000
With Kinner Engine—100 H. P.

SPECIFICATIONS

CAPACITY—
  Pilot and two passengers.

PERFORMANCE WITH NORMAL FULL LOAD
  High speed at sea level............................... 105 M. P. H.
  Landing speed... 43 M. P. H.
  Rate of climb at sea level........................... 500 ft. per min.
  Take-off time, no wind, sea level.................. 11 sec.
  Take-off in feet.. 300 ft.
  Landing run, no brakes............................... 200 ft.
  Climb to 5,000 ft.. 14 min.
  Climb to 10,000 ft...................................... 35 min.
  Service ceiling... 10,000 ft.
  Absolute ceiling... 12,000 ft.
  Cruising speed at 1750 R. P. M.................... 90 M. P. H.
  Normal cruising range (with 42 gal. fuel)....... 400 to 420 miles.

DIMENSIONS—
  Over-all span (tip to tip)............................. 34 ft. 8 in.
  Over-all height... 8 ft. 9 in.
  Over-all length... 24 ft. 8 in.
  Wing chord (upper).................................... 66 in.
  Wing chord (lower).................................... 56 in.
  Wing area.. 296 sq. ft.
  Wing section.. Travel Air No. 1

POWER PLANT—
  Kinner
  100 H. P. at 1800 R. P. M.
  Fuel consumption at cruising speed   8 gal. per hr.
  Wood propeller—stock.
  Adjustable metal propeller, $235.00 extra.

WEIGHTS—
  Gross weight, fully loaded........................... 2300 lbs.
  Weight, empty... 1400 lbs.
  Pay load.. 440 lbs.
  Useful load (2 passengers, pilot, baggage,
    fuel, oil)... 900 lbs.

EQUIPMENT [and other particulars]

COLOR—Fuselage ⎫
  Tail Surfaces   ⎬ Travel Air Blue
  Chassis   ⎪
  Struts   ⎭
  Wings—Orange, or color scheme by arrangement.
UPHOLSTERING—Brown Spanish Leather.
LETTERING—"Travel Air" on fin. Department of Commerce numbers on wings and rudder.
WHEELS—and tires 28x4.
INSTRUMENTS—
  Tachometer   Altimeter
  Oil pressure gauge   Ignition switch
        Starting magneto

LIGHTS—Wired for navigation lights. No lights fitted.

CONTROLS—Single, in rear cockpit. (Dual control, $75.00 extra.)

GAS CAPACITY—42 gallons.

FUEL SUPPLY SYSTEM—Gravity.

PASSENGERS—Two in front cockpit. Pilot in rear cockpit.

CHASSIS—Rubber shock cord in tension.

HEADREST—Standard.

Three-quarter front view

Travel Air Three-place Biplane
Type 3000

Three-quarter rear view

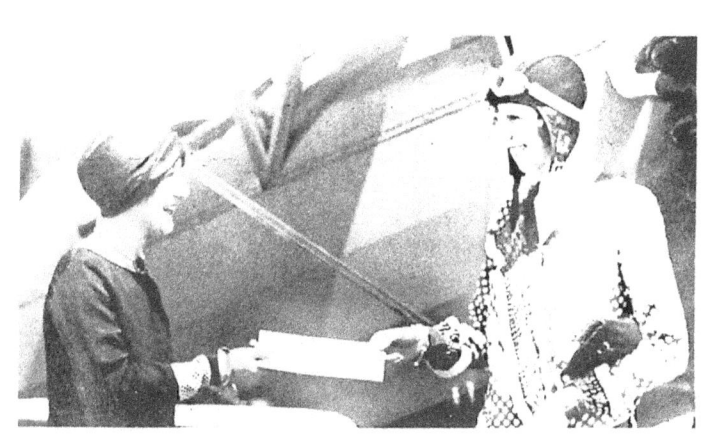

The Travel Air Three-place Biplane
Type 3000
With Hisso Engine

SPECIFICATIONS

CAPACITY—
  Pilot and two passengers.

PERFORMANCE WITH NORMAL FULL LOAD—
  High speed at sea level..................119 M. P. H.
  Landing speed................................46 M. P. H.

DIMENSIONS—
  Over-all span (tip to tip).................34 ft. 8 in.
  Over-all height...................................8 ft. 9 in.
  Over-all length...................................24 ft. 7 in.
  Wing chord (upper)..........................66 in.
  Wing chord (lower)...........................56 in.
  Wing area..296 sq. ft.
  Wing section.....................................Travel Air No. 1

POWER PLANT—
  This plane is built only when customer furnishes his own power plant.

WEIGHTS—
  Gross weight, fully loaded................2590 lbs.
  Weight, empty..................................1640 lbs.
  Useful load..950 lbs.

EQUIPMENT [and other particulars]

COLOR—Fuselage
　　　　Tail Surfaces
　　　　Chassis } Travel Air Blue
　　　　Struts
　　　　Wings—Orange

UPHOLSTERING—Brown Spanish Leather.

LETTERING—"Travel Air" on fin. Department of Commerce numbers on wings and rudder.

WHEELS—and tires 28x4.

INSTRUMENTS—
  Tachometer   Altimeter
  Oil pressure gauge   Ignition switch
  Water temperature thermometer   Choke
          Fuel Pump

LIGHTS—Wings wired for navigation lights. No lights fitted.

CONTROLS—Single, in rear cockpit. (Dual control, $75.00 extra.)

GAS CAPACITY—60 gallons.

TANK LOCATION—In fuselage, forward of passenger cockpit, and center section.

GAS SUPPLY SYSTEM—Gravity from center section.

OIL CAPACITY—5 gallons.

WATER CAPACITY—Approximately 10 gallons.

RADIATOR LOCATION—Underslung.

PASSENGERS—Two in front cockpit. Pilot in rear cockpit.

CHASSIS—Rubber shock cord in tension.

HEADREST—Standard equipment.

The Travel Air Three-place Biplane Type 2000 With OX-5 Engine—90 H. P.

SPECIFICATIONS

CAPACITY—
  Pilot and two passengers.

PERFORMANCE WITH NORMAL FULL LOAD—
  High speed at sea level.................100 M. P. H.
  Landing speed..............................42 M. P. H.
  Normal cruising range (with 42 gal. fuel)....400 to 420 miles

DIMENSIONS—
  Over-all span (tip to tip)   34 ft. 8 in.
  Over-all height   8 ft. 9 in.
  Over-all length   24 ft. 7 in.
  Wing chord (upper)   66 in.
  Wing chord (lower) ....56 in.
  Wing area................................296 sq. ft.
  Wing section............................Travel Air No. 1

POWER PLANT—
  *Curtiss OX-5.
  90 H. P. at 1450 R. P. M.
  Fuel consumption at cruising speed...........8 gal. per hr.
  Hamilton or Hartzell wood propeller.

WEIGHTS—
  Gross weight, fully loaded.............2180 lbs.
  Weight, empty............................1335 lbs.

EQUIPMENT [and other particulars]

COLOR—Fuselage ⎫
  Tail Surfaces ⎬ Travel Air Blue
  Chassis ⎪
  Struts ⎭
  Wings— Aluminum

UPHOLSTERING—Fabrikoid.

LETTERING—"Travel Air" on fin. Department of Commerce numbers on wings and rudder.

WHEELS—and tires 28x4.

INSTRUMENTS—
  Tachometer   Altimeter
  Oil pressure gauge   Ignition switch
  Water temperature thermometer   Choke

LIGHTS—Wings wired for navigation lights. No lights fitted.

CONTROLS—Single, in rear cockpit. (Dual control, $75.00 extra.)

GAS CAPACITY—42 gallons.

TANK LOCATION—In fuselage, forward of passenger cockpit.

GAS SUPPLY SYSTEM—Gravity.

OIL CAPACITY—4 gallons in motor.

WATER CAPACITY—Approximately 5 gallons.

RADIATOR LOCATION—Underslung.

PASSENGERS—Two in front cockpit. Pilot in rear cockpit.

CHASSIS—Rubber shock cord in tension.

HEADREST—Standard equipment.

*NOTE—This ship can also be equipped with OXX6 motor.

Flying With Travel Air

Scarcely a day passes, but that some Travel Air, someplace in the world, distinguishes itself by outstanding performance, and brings new satisfaction to its owner.

Daily throughout the year prospective purchasers of airplanes come to the factory to see the enormous manufacturing facilities, to take demonstrations, and "take off" for home in the Travel Air plane best suited for their needs. Nor is it uncommon for Eastern purchasers to meet Western buyers on Travel Air field with Northern prospects and Southern enthusiasts, joining in the satisfaction of coming to the exact geographical center of the U. S. to fly home the Travel Air model of their choice.

Almost daily, often hourly, during the day, telegrams are received at the Travel Air offices enthusiastically reporting the stability, the flying qualities and the economy of operation of their Travel Air.

The Travel Air files of correspondence grow daily in size with gratifying letters, pictures and testimonials sent by owners as an appreciation of their enthusiasm over Travel Air performance. It is manifestly impossible to reproduce all of these in this book. Those appearing on these pages are, however, typical of nation—yes world-wide acceptance of

TRAVEL AIR
the
Standard of Aircraft Comparison

Louise M'Phetridge von Thaden—A pioneer in the establishment of world's altitude and sustained flight records for women. In December, 1928 attained an altitude of 25,400 feet, altimeter reading, using a stock model Hisso Travel Air. In March, 1929 established a flight endurance record of 21 hours, 3 minutes, 12 seconds in a Hisso Travel Air.

Travel Air planes in flight over San Francisco Bay, the scene of Mrs. von Thaden's altitude and sustained flight attempts.

San Francisco to Honolulu in 26 Hours

The flyers were due. For hours a vast crowd had waited on the beach—eagerly—anxiously—eyes searching over the vast expanse of ocean, for the first glimse of the intrepid airmen who had left San Francisco the day before.

Then a rapidly moving speck appeared in the distant sky. Someone pointed to it. All faces turned quickly to see. Soon was heard the roar of a powerful motor, and Art Goebel glided down to the beach of a strange shore—the winner on the Dole San Francisco-Hawaii flight, in 26 hours over the 2,497 mile uncharted course.

Art Goebel's ship—The Woolaroc—Travel Air built—had met every exacting demand made upon it during the long hours of daylight and darkness—fog, wind, rain and sunshine, with only the vast ocean below.

To appreciate the full significance of this remarkable flight, one must remember the complete confidence placed by Art Goebel in the airplane in which he was to shoot at a mere speck of an island in the Pacific ocean, almost 2500 miles from San Francisco and with a gasoline capacity of less than 100 more miles.

This famous flight brought to The Travel Air Company an even greater appreciation of the need of stability and the necessity of making air planes that would "fly themselves," so to speak. Ships with these characteristics and equipped with first class flying and navigation instruments have made flying safe and built up a steadily increasing confidence on the part of pilots and the general public.

The epoch making flight of Art Goebel in the Woolaroc is but one of hundreds of Travel Air achievements in speed, endurance and altitude contests in wind storm and fair weather.

Travel Air makes it an unvarying policy to obtain first handed, reliable information on the performance of Travel Air planes in such events. This policy, as well as keeping constantly in touch with Travel Air owners, makes it possible to build into every Travel Air leaving the factory, the experience of all Travel Airs now in use.

Col. Arthur C. Goebel, winner of the Dole San Francisco-Hawaii flight in August, 1927.

The Woolaroc, Travel Air built and Wright engine powered, equipped with radio and every practical instrument then known to aerial navigation, photographed after one of its trial flights before taking off for Honolulu.

The famous Wallace Beery smile and characteristic pose were faithfully caught by the camera when this well-known Famous Lasky star came to the Travel Air factory to fly away his new Luxury Cabin Travel Air Monoplane—Wasp powered, luxuriously upholstered and lavatory equipped. This is "Wally's" second Travel Air—the first being a Whirlwind Biplane. Beery holds a transport pilot's license.

Travel Air planes have always been characterized by their ability to safely "sit down" and take off from small fields, in either high or low altitudes. C. B. Cosgrove, Phoenix, Arizona, kindly furnishes us with convincing photographic proof of this outstanding Travel Air performance.

The Phillips Petroleum Company find this attribute of the greatest value in using their Travel Air Cabin Monoplane.

The ship above is the property of the Anchorage Air Transport, Inc., of Anchorage, Alaska. It is used extensively during the fur season for transporting furs into Anchorage for shipment South. This photo shows it being lowered into the water for a trip to a distant post. On its return it carried in some $18,000.00 worth of raw fur.

The Anchorage Air Transport operates two Travel Air biplanes, both equipped to use either pontoons or skiis for summer or winter flying.

Below is a Travel Air taking off for a practice flight from Travel Air field—a scene that never loses the interest of the airminded. Many people gather at the field each day to watch these short flights.

Leading movie directors have, for years, shown a preference for the use of Travel Air planes in the making of exciting pictures for the silver screen. Qualities of performance with dependability, speed, maneuverability and safety are of especial importance in the filming of a picture, when the cameras are "clicking" and the entire cast "on location."

Notable among the famous pictures in which Travel Air planes have been used are "The Air Circus" and "Hell's Angels." The photograph at the left is of Arthur Lake ready to "take off" and fly in one of the scenes in "The Air Circus."

Below is a photo of Richard E. James, seventeen year old Flushing, New York, school boy beside the Travel Air in which he won the $1,000.00 prize offered by the American Society for the Promotion of Aviation to the first youth under eithteen to cross the continent, "solo" in an airplane.

At the right is Victor Fleming, famous movie director standing beside the door of his new Travel Air Cabin Monoplane just after its arrival in Hollywood by air from Wichita. Mr. Fleming is a pilot of long experience.

The Harvard Flying Club has gained such favor with Harvard undergraduates that today there is a long waiting list of applications for membership. Travel Air planes were selected shortly after its organization, and are used exclusively for both dual instruction and solo flights.

It appears that the organization of this famous club started something. All over the country, colleges and universities are forming similar clubs—and in most instances their choice of training ships is Travel Air.

Also several large groups of private individuals for sake of economy have banded themselves into flying organizations. Here too, Travel Air predominates.

Around the pylon and first across the finish line—a Travel Air. Somewhere in the country almost every day, scenes like the one on the left occur.

The photo shown here is very unusual, snapped of a Travel Air biplane as it rounded a pylon in a recent flying meet. Notice that the judges have fled to safety from their post at the pylon.

This picture shows very definitely the responsiveness of Travel Airs to their controls. No pilot would have executed such a manoeuvre without supreme confidence in the ship he was flying—confidence that his ship respond instantly to every control.

The photo below is of Billy Parker standing beside his second Travel Air. Mr. Parker is Director of the Aeronautical Activities of the Phillips Petroleum Company, manufacturers of a well known Aviation Gasoline, Phillips "66". Travel Air planes have carried Mr. Parker thousands of miles on business transactions.

Putting the Travel Air to a very practical use. The photo above shows two combines at work in a Western wheat field. The picture below shows a pilot delivering needed repairs to them—delivered without delay. During the harvest season on the plains Travel Air is very frequently put to this and similar uses in servicing harvesting equipment to avoid unnecessary lost time and delays.

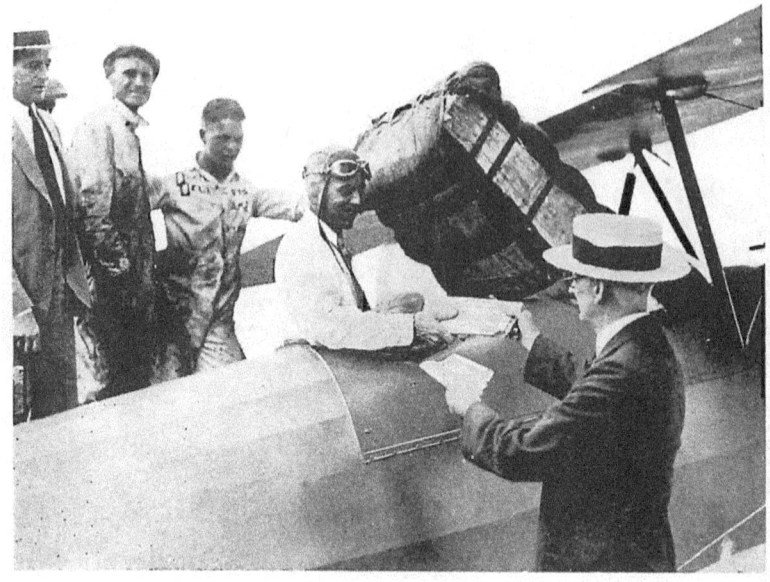

New York market.

In the lower left is shown Mr. E. H. McReynolds, Assistant to the President of the Missouri Pacific Rail Road, as he accepted delivery on a Whirlwind powered Travel Air biplane. Mr. Reynolds is on the right in this photo. The ship was the first purchased by a railroad for its own individual use.

The lower right is Col. Lindbergh standing beside the Travel Air Monoplane in which he flew to Mexico to visit Anne Morrow. The Colonel started for Mexico in his own biplane, but after arriving in Kansas City, decided on a Travel Air Cabin Monoplane to complete the trip. Arranging details by long distance phone he flew to Mexico in comfort and security.

No wonder cotton "went up." Above is a 430 pound bale of cotton being loaded into a Travel Air biplane belonging to Doug Davis. This bale of cotton was flown from Georgia to New York in the Travel Air, and was auctioned on the

Above is a typical scene enacted daily on many airports throughout America—the loading of passengers, enroute to distant cities, in safe, new Travel Air Monoplanes.

On a great many of the chartered airlines engaged in passenger transportation, Travel Air Monoplanes are exclusive equipment. The ship's sturdy appearance at once gains the confidence of the passengers. The luxurious interior invites complete relaxation for a swift, comfortable ride through the clouds to any destination. This feeling of comfortable security has won thousands of friends to Travel Air among the patrons of air lines.

Recognizing this "passenger acceptance" of Travel Air each month finds new names among operators using Travel Air equipment exclusively.

Below is Wilbur D. Mays, prominent Los Angeles merchant photographed beside his Travel Air Monoplane shortly after it's arrival by air in Los Angeles.

The movie producers to which Ken Maynard is under contract, feared for his safety in flying. Ken allayed their fears with the purchase of a Travel Air—now everyone is happy.

No better evidence of the public confidence in Travel Air could be offered than the telegram from Tom Hardin, shown below.

```
W7 F 229P 13   3EXA FT WORTH TEX APRIL 19 1929
WALTER BEECH=
     TRAVEL AIR MFG CO  WICHITA KANSAS=


BUILD ME WHATEVER YOU THINK I OUGHT TO HAVE REGARDS=


                         TOM HARDIN TEXAS AIR TRANSPORT
OK G.
```

Melbourne, Australia, October 4, 1928.—It will interest you to know that the Travel Air OX-5 job ran in second place at a recent aerial derby held here—just beaten by a 375 hp. DH4. Its official average speed was 105 m. p. h. carrying a pilot and two passengers. Photo is enclosed showing the machine at finish of race. Major H. deHaviland has flown this machine and likes it very much.   May 27, 1929.—The Travel Air, I imported last year has proven satisfactory. Now has well over 200 hours.—W. Raymond Garrett.

These two planes were recently shipped to "Westpat," Honolulu. The photograph shows the method of boxing for ocean shipment.

Nation Wide Distribution Through These Distributors and Dealers

ALABAMA
   T. A. T. FLYING SERVICE, INC., Fort Worth, Texas.

ARIZONA
   SOUTHWEST AIR SERVICE, INC., Tucson, Arizona. (Municipal Airport).
      AERO CORPORATION OF ARIZONA, Phoenix, Ariz.

ARKANSAS (Northeastern part)
   T. A. T. FLYING SERVICE, INC.,
      VALLEY AIR LINES, INC., P. O. Box 2238, Memphis, Tenn.

CALIFORNIA
   H. C. LIPPIATT, 506 N. Crescent Heights Blvd., Hollywood, Cal.
      SAN DIEGO AIR SERVICE CORP., Lindbergh Field, San Diego, Cal.
   D C. WARREN CO., 970 Geary St., San Francisco, Calif.
      WESTERN AIRLINES, Santa Rosa Airport, Calif.
      HUMBOLDT FLYING SERVICE, Eureka Airport, Calif.
      LIND'S AIRPORT, Lodi, Calif.
      GAUDIN & PAHL, Tulare, Calif.
      ROSS & GRISWOLD, Visalia Airport, Calif.
      ALLEN & NIGHTINGALE, Stockton Airport, Calif.
      INTERSTATE AIRLINES, Inc., Richmond Airport, Calif.
      INGVALD FAUERSKOU, Sacramento Airport, Calif.
      SAN BENITO FLYING SCHOOL, Turner Field, Hollister, Cal.

COLORADO
   TRAVEL AIRWAYS, INC., 7 Tejon Street, Colorado Springs, Colo.

FLORIDA
   McMULLEN AIRCRAFT COMPANY, (McMullen Airport) Tampa, Florida.

GEORGIA
   T. A. T. FLYING SERVICE, INC., Fort Worth, Texas.
      DOUGLAS H. DAVIS, Agent, Candler Field, Atlanta, Ga.

IDAHO
   UNION PACIFIC AIRWAYS, INC., Airport, Ogden, Utah. (Southern part of Idaho).

ILLINOIS
   FRED MACHNEY, 1828 Douglas St., Rockford, Ill. (N. W. Ill.)
   LA SALLE-PERU AIRWAYS, INC., La Salle, Illinois. (East Central, Ill.)
   CONTINENTAL AIR SERVICE, INC., 2420 So. Park Way, Chicago, Ill. (N. E. Ill.)
      ARTHUR C. CHESTER, Joliet Airport, Joliet, Ill.
   QUINCY AIRCRAFT CORPORATION, Quincy, Ill. (West Central, Ill.)
   ROBERTSON AIRCRAFT CORP., St. Louis, Mo. (Southern Ill.)

IOWA
   MID-WEST AVIATION CORP., 318 S. 19th St., Omaha, Nebr.
      MID-WEST AVIATION CORP., Council Bluffs, Iowa.
      MID-WEST AVIATION CORP., Des Moines, Iowa.
      KARI-KEEN SCHOOL OF AVIATION, Leeds, Sioux City, Iowa.

INDIANA
   HOOSIER AIRPORT CORPORATION, Hoosier Airport, Indianapolis, Ind.
      THE SILVER FOX AVIATION CO., Muncie, Ind.
      THE BEACON SCHOOL OF AVIATION, Gary, Ind.

KANSAS
   ROY E. MORRIS AIRCRAFT CORP., Topeka, Kans. (E. C. Kansas)
   TRUMAN WADLOW, Box 666, St. Joseph, Mo. (N. E. Kansas)

KENTUCKY
   HOOSIER AIRPORT CORP., Hoosier Airport, Indianapolis, Ind.
   WATSON AIRPORT CORP., Blue Ash, Ohio.
      A. S. BOYER, Alexander, Ky.

LOUISIANA
   DELTA AIR SERVICE, INC., Ouachita Nat'l Bank Bldg., Monroe, La.
      CLEM S. CLARKE, Shreveport, La.

MAINE
   EAST COAST AIRCRAFT SALES CORP., 94 Ames Bldg., Boston, Mass.
      AMERICAN AIRPORTS CORP. OF NEW ENGLAND, 805 Statler Bldg., Boston, Mass. (Dealer for state of Maine)

MASSACHUSETTS
   EAST COAST AIRCRAFT SALES CORP., 94 Ames Bldg., Boston, Mass.
      RUSSELL N. BOARDMAN, 94 Ames Bldg., Boston, Mass. (Dealer for E. Cape Cod District)
      KEELEY-KING AIRCRAFT CORPORATION, Taunton, Mass.

MICHIGAN
   SKF AIR SERVICE, INC., Lansing, Mich.
   FURNITURE CAPITAL AIR SERVICE, 702 Trust Bldg., Grand Rapids, Mich.
      GRAND HAVEN AIR SERVICE, Grand Haven, Mich.

MINNESOTA
   MID-WEST AVIATION CORP., 318 S. 19th St., Omaha, Nebr.

MISSOURI
   ROBERTSON AIRCRAFT CORP., Anglum, Mo.
   TRAVEL AIR SALES, INC., 413 West Walnut St., Springfield, Mo. (South Central part of the State)
      McCLUER AIR SERVICE, Springfield, Mo.

MISSISSIPPI
   T. A. T. FLYING SERVICE, INC., Fort Worth, Texas. (Northern Half of State)
      VALLEY AIR LINES, INC., P. O. Box 2238, Memphis, Tenn.
   E. J. MOSER, Jr., Meridian, Miss. (Southern Half of State)

MONTANA
   BUTTE AIRCRAFT CORP. 2428 So. Montana St., Butte, Mont.
      JOHNSON FLYING SERVICE, Missoula, Mont.
      FRANK WILEY, Miles City, Mont.
      H H AND C AIRWAYS, Harlowton, Mont.
      ANACONDA AIR SERVICE, Anaconda, Mont.

NEBRASKA
   MID-WEST AVIATION CORP., 318 So. 19th Street, Omaha, Nebr.
      WALT-SMITH SCHOOL OF AVIATION, Grand Island, Nebr.
      FREMONT AIRCRAFT CORP., Fremont, Nebr.
      NORFOLK FLYING SCHOOL, Norfolk, Nebr.

NEW HAMPSHIRE
   EAST COAST AIRCRAFT SALES CORP., 94 Ames Bldg., Boston, Mass.
      NEW HAMPSHIRE AVIATION & MARINE CORP., Concord, N. H.

NEW JERSEY
   N. R. AIRWAYS, 220 Front Street, Mineola, L. I., N. Y.
      NEWARK AIR SERVICE, Newark Airport, Newark, N. J.

NEW MEXICO
   SOUTHWEST AIR SERVICE, INC., Tucson, Arizona.

NEW YORK
   FLYERS INC., 399 State Street, Albany, N. Y.
      CENTRAL NEW YORK AIRWAYS INC., Norwich, N. Y.
      EMPIRE AIR TRANSPORT, INC., 701 Loew Bldg., Syracuse, N. Y.
      GLOVE CITY AIRWAYS, INC., Gloversville, N. Y.
   Wm. H. EMERY, Jr., Bradford, Penn. (Western New York)
      WRIGHT & ESENWEIN, Buffalo Airport, Buffalo, N. Y.
   WARD S. LENT, Poughkeepsie, N. Y.
   N. R. AIRWAYS, INC., 220 Front St., Mineola, L. I., N. Y.

NORTH DAKOTA
   CANFIELD FLYING SERVICE, Williston, N. D.
      FARGO AVIATION CO., Fargo, N. D.

Nation Wide Distribution Through These Distributors and Dealers

OHIO

LITTLE-GREINER FLYING SERVICE, INC., Loganda Citizens National Bank Bldg., Springfield, Ohio.
- Greenville Aircraft, Inc., Lansdown Airport, Greenville, Ohio.

LOGAN AVIATION COMPANY, 716 West Superior Ave., Cleveland, Ohio.
- Swaney Aircraft Corp., East Liverpool, Ohio.
- Geo. Whysall & Associates, Marion, Ohio.

WATSON AIRPORT, INC., Blue Ash, Ohio.
- Robert E. Clifton, c/o Fulflo Specialties Co., Blanchester, Ohio.
- Dixie Davis Flying Field, Inc., Union Levee, Cincinnati, Ohio.

OKLAHOMA

CENTRAL AIRLINES COMPANY, P. O. Box 3212, Tulsa, Okla.

OREGON

HOBI AIRWAYS COMPANY, INC., Eugene, Oregon.
- Everly School of Aeronautics, Salem Airport, Salem, Ore.
- Shields-Clark Flying Service, Swan Island, Portland, Ore.

PENNSYLVANIA

Wm. H. Emery Jr., Bradford, Penn. (N. W. part of state)
- Aeronautical Service Corp., 9th & Peach, Erie, Pa.

ALLENTOWN AVIATION CORP., Allentown, Penn.

PITTSBURGH AIRPLANE SALES CORP., Pittsburgh, Penn. (S. W. part of state)

WILKES-BARRE WYOMING VALLEY AIRPORT CORP., Wilkes-Barre, Pa. (N. E. part of state)

SOUTH DAKOTA

CANFIELD FLYING SERVICE, Williston, N. D.
- C. J. Wage, Ferney, So. Dakota.
- Dakota Airplane Co., Aberdeen, So. Dakota.

RHODE ISLAND

EAST COAST AIRCRAFT SALES CORP., 94 Ames Bldg., Boston, Mass.

TENNESSEE

T. A. T. FLYING SERVICE, Fort Worth, Texas.
- Douglas H. Davis, Agent eastern part of state, Candler Field, Atlanta, Ga.
- Valley Air Lines, Inc., P. O. Box 2238, Memphis, Tenn. (Western part of state)

TEXAS

T. A. T. FLYING SERVICE, INC., Fort Worth Nat'l Bank Bldg., Fort Worth, Texas.
- L. T. Hammond, Wichita Falls, Texas.
- L. H. Plain, Lubbock, Texas.
- Harold Nichols, Corsicana, Texas.
- C. A. Nietern, Brownsville, Texas.

UTAH

UNION PACIFIC AIRWAYS, INC., Airport, Ogden, Utah.
- Thompson Flying Service, Airport, Salt Lake City, Utah.

WASHINGTON

HOBI AIRWAYS COMPANY, INC., Aberdeen, Wash.
- The Coast Airlines, Boeing Field, Seattle, Wash.

WEST VIRGINIA

PITTSBURGH AIRPLANE SALES CORP., 4740 Baum Blvd., Pittsburgh, Pa.

WISCONSIN

MID-WEST AIR TRANSPORT CO., Madison Airport, Madison, Wisconsin.
- Beloit Airways, Inc., Beloit, Wisconsin.
- Cash Chamberlain, County Airport, Milwaukee, Wisconsin.
- Head of the Lakes Airways, Superior, Wisconsin.
- Eau Claire, Airways, Eau Claire, Wisconsin.
- LaCross Aviation Co., LaCross, Wisconsin.

WYOMING

CHEYENNE AIR SERVICE, INC., 1723 Capitol Ave., Cheyenne, Wyo.

FOREIGN REPRESENTATIVES

AEREO EXPORT COMPANY, 304 Orpheum Bldg., Wichita, Kansas. West Indies, Central and South America.

ANDERSON, MEYER & COMPANY, 79 Madison Ave., New York, N. Y. 18 provinces of China, Manchuria, Mongolia, Chinese Turkestan Thibet, the Island of Hongkong and leased territories.

CONTINENTAL AERO CORPORATION, LTD., 825 Confederation Bldg., Montreal, Eastern Canada.

W. RAYMOND GARRETT, 42 Clarendon Street, South Melbourne, Australia. Australia and New Zeland.

K. K. HOFFMAN, c/o E. L. Buckley, Apartado 260, Tampico, Mexico. Mexico.

CALVIN MARTIN, P. O. Box 1341, Cape Town, South Africa. South Africa.

SIMMONS AIRCRAFT EXPORT DIVISION, Steel Incorporated, Chamber of Commerce Bldg., Los Angeles, Calif. Territory: Siberia, India, Siam, Netherlands, East Indies, Korea, Japan, Greece, Poland, Rumania, Italy.

WESTERN PACIFIC AIR TRANSPORT, INC., Honolulu, Hawaii. Hawaiian and Philippine Islands.

The Standard of Aircraft Comparison
TRAVEL AIR COMPANY
WICHITA, KANSAS

The MYSTERY SHIP

LOW WING TRAVEL AIR
MODEL R

Travel Air "Mystery Ship"

Low Wing Model R

A famous pilot once remarked that, given sufficient power, a barn door could be flown. Pursuing this strange concept and allowing a barn door the ordinary dimensions of 10 by 12½ feet, one finds that it coincides exactly in surface area with the wings of the Travel Air "Mystery Ship"—125 square feet, which, with "sufficient" power in the form of the special Wright Whirlwind J-6 Engine, carries this remarkable ship through the air at a speed of 235 miles per hour!

Here the comparison ceases, for this Travel Air Low Wing Monoplane is an example of the highest refinement of Curtiss-Wright engineering leadership.

Built for experimental purposes, the Model R was completed in August 1929 and first publicly exhibited when it was flown from the Travel Air factory at Wichita, Kansas, to the National Air Races at Cleveland. The nickname, "Mystery Ship" was given the plane when it was rumored at the Cleveland meet that Travel Air was to enter a new ship of amazing speed and performance.

The "Mystery" abundantly fulfilled advance rumors by daily thrilling the crowds with its astonishing maneuvers. Flown by Douglas H. Davis, famous pilot and Curtiss-Wright Regional Sales Manager, the "Mystery Ship" did a string of loops and slow rolls, both horizontally and upward, that gave spectators a new idea of flying evolutions to which a commercial craft may be put.

The outstanding feature of the National Air Races of 1929 was the free-for-all race in which seven planes, including one representative each from the Army and Navy, were entered. The sensational victor of this race was the Travel Air "Mystery Ship."

An average speed of 194.9 m.p.h. was turned in by the Travel Air, and this was achieved despite the accidental cutting of a pylon which necessitated turning back to round the mark correctly. The elapsed time for the 50 mile race was 14 min., 05.9 seconds. On the fastest lap the "Mystery Ship" was clocked at 208.69 m.p.h.

This was the highest speed ever achieved by a commercial plane in the United States, and far exceeded the best time made by any machine, either commercial or military, throughout the races. This was also the first time in history that a commercial plane defeated both the Army and Navy in a free-for-all race.

A high compliment paid to the perfection of the "Mystery Ship" is the fact that a duplicate plane was ordered by the Shell Aviation Corporation for the use of Lieut. James H. Doolittle, generally recognized by the world of aviation as the greatest all-around aeronautical engineer and test pilot in the world.

Lieutenant Doolittle, winner of the 1925 Schneider Cup Race, is now in Chicago on Aviation activities of the Shell Petroleum Company and will probably use the "Mystery Ship" to achieve new civilian records just as he has set many military records.

That the "Mystery Ship" will help him do this is evidenced by the recent epoch-making flight of Douglas H. Davis. After breakfasting in New York, Mr. Davis flew to Atlanta in time for lunch—*making this 800 mile trip in 4½ hours.*

Such amazing performance has been made possible by many radical departures from usual design. The outstanding of these is the unusually small wing surfaces which are of plywood constructed of spruce, Haskelite and mahogany. Wings are tapered from fuselage to tips, and in addition to their connection with stubs projecting 25 inches from fuselage are braced with streamline wires to landing gear and to the cabane which is concealed beneath the cowling.

The special Wright Whirlwind R-975 engine, which develops approximately 400 H.P. at 2,300 M.P.H. is surrounded by a venturi cowling. Fuselage is of chrome molybdenum steel tubing braced throughout. It is wedge-shaped . . . providing ample room, yet offering as little frontal resistance as possible.

The fairing and turtle deck are of spruce superstructure and are also covered with mahogany plywood. The trim lines, giving the utmost in streamlining, are enhanced by a highly polished finish.

Landing gear is a unique combination of oil and coil spring devices—an oil cylinder to absorb the initial shock of landing and spring to absorb the shocks of taxying. The wheels and all landing gear mechanism are enclosed in aluminum fairing.

Although no definite plans have been made to put this model into regular production, Travel Air will gladly provide further detailed information to those who are interested Write Dept. TDM 1 for particulars.

LIEUT. JAMES H. DOOLITTLE who says "The Travel Air Mystery Ship is beyond question the fine airplane that I have ever flown.

Specifications
"THE MYSTERY SHIP"

Power plant . . J-6 300 H.P., or J-6 225 H.P. Wright Whirlwind Engine
Class . . . . Open Low Wing Monoplane

Capacity

Passenger.	1 pilot
Gross Weight.	1,940 lbs.
Disposable Load.	465 lbs.
Weight Empty.	1,475 lbs.
Fuel Capacity.	47 Gal.
Oil Capacity.	6 Gal.

Dimensions

Span Overall.	29 Ft. 2 In.
Length.	20 Ft. 2 In.
Height.	7 Ft. 9 In.
Wing Cord.	5 Ft.
Wing Area.	125 Sq. Ft.
Wing Loading (Lbs. per Sq. Ft.)	15.5
Power Loading (Lbs. per H.P.)	4.6

Performance

High Speed.	235 M.P.H.
Cruising Speed.	150 M.P.H.
Landing Speed.	70 M.P.H.
Rate of Climb.	3,200 F.P.M.
Service Ceiling.	30,000 Ft.
Absolute Ceiling.	31,000 Ft.
Cruising Range.	525 Mi.

Standard Equipment

Canvas Cockpit and Propeller Covers.

TRAVEL AIR COMPANY
Division of CURTISS-WRIGHT
Sales Offices: 27 West 57th Street, New York

They *flew*— they *saw*— they *concurred*

A DECISION was needed—urgently. The successful completion of a huge project was at stake. The directors, hurriedly summoned, decided to see conditions for themselves. Boarding their private Travel Air they flew— they saw, they concurred.

Modern Caesars of industry, responsible for the direction of vast and far-flung properties, are turning more and more to the airplane as a means of quick, personal contact with their forces in the field. At short notice and in a few hours of flying time, they can make tours of inspection which otherwise might take weeks—or even not be made at all.

The six passenger Travel Air cabin monoplane is particularly well suited for the modern flying directorate or executive committee. Powered with the 300 Horse Power Wright Whirlwind engine, it has a cruising speed of 115 m.p.h., a high speed of 135. A more luxurious model, equipped with a 420 h.p. engine is available. Either can be equipped with office furnishings to suit the purchaser.

A nationwide organization of Curtiss-Wright distributors and a network of more than forty Curtiss-Wright bases strategically located, assure prompt service to the users of Travel Air planes wherever they may fly.

Low Operating Cost. Full particulars of the actual use of Travel Air planes in business, with rather surprising figures as to low operating cost, will be gladly supplied. Executives can receive this information by writing department T-1.

TRAVEL AIR COMPANY
Division of CURTISS-WRIGHT
Sales Offices: 27 West 57th Street, New York

A PLANE FOR EVERY PURPOSE   **TRAVEL AIR**

THE STANDARD OF AIRCRAFT COMPARISON

SKYWARD

Haven't you been imbued with the spirit of adventure; to see mother earth from the sky; to peer down into the heart of a rustling city with her millions at work and play; or scan the lakes dotted with moving vessels or perhaps look into the depths of a forest where flow the rippling streams; or even into the mountains where peaks reach heavenward with majestic splendor?

Is habit keeping you out of the air? Is your first flight still in the future? Shake off the shackles of ultra-conservatism and take the skyroad to new and thrilling adventures. Let the earth become your stepping stone to the limitless reaches of the sky.

Your first feel of the air will convince—establish complete confidence in the stability and ease of flying an airplane.

The steadily increasing confidence in Travel Air performance with dependability is conclusively proven by the fact that over one thousand Travel Air planes are in daily use for business or pleasure.

Flying demonstrations, without obligations, may be had by appointment with any of the 127 Travel Air distributors, all strategically located.

Catalog illustrating and describing three types of dual control cabin monoplanes, seating four and six passengers, and eight types of three-seated open cockpit biplanes gladly sent free on request. Write department M-10.

TRAVEL AIR COMPANY
WICHITA, KANSAS

MAKES A MINUTE MEAN TWO MILES IN CUSHIONED EASE AND COMFORT!

THE TRAVEL AIR
SPORTSMAN

The racy new 3-place TRAVEL AIR *Sportsman* is a rugged, 2-miles-a-minute performer which rides with the ease and comfort of a touring car! ● Smoothly it glides down the runway...leaps skyward within 150 yards...climbs 750 feet a minute...levels off...strikes 120 m.p.h. if you wish...and with the endurance of its record-holding Challenger engine cruises easily over 600 miles in six hours! ● The sturdy *Sportsman* is an able sky rider and a cozy carrier for three because Curtiss-Wright designers, knowing what private pilots prefer, have put into this craft the progressive devices taken from their long experience in building many types of planes. ● It floats in and lands at 48 m.p.h. Special TRAVEL AIR shock absorbers, and split-axle undercarriage eliminate the shock of careless landings on rough fields. Internal expanding brakes assure ground control. The entire fuselage structure is made of strong alloy steel. Wide wings give you easy, sure, stable control. Convenience of seats, controls, instruments, and fittings—even to strap-cradle for extra luggage—make the *Sportsman* as comfortable as a car. ● Here is *your* plane, your *personal* craft. See your Curtiss-Wright dealer for a demonstration and you'll want to fly the *Sportsman* away!

CURTISS-WRIGHT
AIRPLANE COMPANY
ROBERTSON, MISSOURI

FACTORIES: ST. LOUIS, MO.   WICHITA, KANSAS

STABLE FOR SPORT
STURDY FOR TRAINING

THE TRAVEL AIR
"SPORT-TRAINER"

WHAT Curtiss-Wright learned from the "Mystery Ship," fastest commercial plane in the world, Curtiss-Wright now incorporates in the striking new TRAVEL AIR Sport-Trainer. ● Sturdily built, trimly refined, you'll like this fleet little ship. It offers advances in stability, handling and servicing ease, which can be affected only when an organization builds for the whole field. ● Its clean-cut lines, its sleek streamlining, its speed in excess of 100 m.p.h. and cruising range of 500 miles, make it a craft of which you may be justly proud. ● Actually it's so stable in flight and so responsive to all controls that it's a real treat to fly it! ● Powered with the air-cooled Wright-Gipsy engine, with a full complement of quality instruments, with a special wide-tread, shock-absorbing landing gear and brakes, this TRAVEL AIR is remarkably easy to control on the ground or in the air. In every detail it is designed to make flying and servicing by the owner as inexpensive as possible. ● That's why the Sport-Trainer will make a wide appeal to 1931 buyers!

CURTISS-WRIGHT
AIRPLANE COMPANY
ROBERTSON, MISSOURI

NOW TRAVEL AIR

Comfort, safety, economy at unusually low prices

TYPE 4-D, powered with J-6 225 H.P. Wright Whirlwind engine—speed up to 132 M.P.H.—ceiling 16,500 ft.—cruising range 550 miles.

TYPE E-4000, powered with J-6 165 H.P. Wright Whirlwind engine—speed up to 122 M.P.H.—ceiling 14,500 ft.—cruising range 690 miles.

TYPE 2000, powered with Curtiss OX5 90 H.P. engine—speed up to 100 M.P.H.—ceiling 12,000 ft.—cruising range 420 miles.

MANY operators have discovered that the Travel Air biplane is the ideal ship for training, passenger hopping, taxi and charter service. They have found that its features of safety, comfort and economy mean maximum profit from their investment.

The Travel Air biplane is powered with 165 h.p., 225 h.p., or 300 h.p. Wright Whirlwinds, Curtiss OX5, Warner Scarab, Axelson, Kinner, etc.—at the owner's option. It is versatile, easily-handled, trustworthy. The name "Travel Air" guarantees an inherent sturdiness that assures dependability, laughs at hard knocks and defies the greatest strains—a well-built, comfortable plane embodying the last word in safety and ease of flying.

In the past, surprisingly low costs have been outstanding features of Travel Air superiority. Now, due to manufacturing economies brought about by Curtiss-Wright, the same low upkeep, rugged strength and splendid performance of Travel Air biplanes, are offered at exceptionally low initial prices. You are invited to share in these savings. Prices, depending on the engine desired, start as low as $2195, with down payments as low as $750.

Operating better ships means increased profits to you. Low prices of Travel Air put both within easy reach. Write today for full information. Address Department T-71 Sales Division, Curtiss-Wright Corporation, 27 W. 57th St., New York.

CURTISS-WRIGHT
CORPORATION

Theirs is a *Ten-day Week*

THE five-day week may be the thing for labor, but what most executives need today is a ten-day week. A conference in Toronto, an appointment in Wheeling, W. Va., the weekly meeting of the factory committee in Evansville, Ind., a three-day trade convention at Atlantic City. Now it can be done, easily, comfortably, in one week—the new Travel Air ten-day week for major executives.

* * * *

An increasing number of progressive concerns are using the six-passenger Travel Air cabin plane to transport their directors and executive officers on missions of importance. Swiftly and safely, Travel Air carries them cross country with a minimum of time out for travel. Powered with a 300 h. p. Wright Whirlwind engine, this luxuriously furnished monoplane has a cruising speed of 110 m. p. h., a range of 430 miles. Another model, powered with a 420 h. p. engine, flies even faster and farther.

No matter where their business may take them, owners of Travel Air planes have the great advantage of never being far from the service facilities of Travel Air distributors and Curtiss-Wright airports. Over forty of these landing fields are strategically located throughout the country.

* * * *

Cost of Operation. Tabulations of the cost of operating business planes, based on actual experience of prominent firms, will be supplied to interested executives. For these, and for full information regarding the performance of Travel Air planes, write department T70.

TRAVEL AIR COMPANY
Division of CURTISS-WRIGHT
27 WEST 57TH STREET · NEW YORK

A PLANE FOR EVERY PURPOSE *TRAVEL AIR*

TRAVEL AIR SAVES TIME

for the world's largest makers of time-saving tools

INDUSTRY sets a new pace. It was therefore a natural development that Black & Decker, the world's largest makers of portable electric tools, chose the Travel Air Six-place Cabin Monoplane to bring their extensive sales territories into closely supervised unity.

In January, the Black & Decker Travel Air was sent on a 38-day tour through eight southeastern states. District managers accompanied the salesman-pilot through each territory. Important sales and a new assurance of service were the result.

Time-saving! Golden words to great business organizations. Sturdy! Travel Air is designed and engineered by the world's oldest and largest airplane manufacturing organization. Reliable! Wind and weather hold no difficulties for Travel Air steadiness and supreme maneuverability. Fast! Wright-powered with 300 h. p. Whirlwind engine; speed up to 135 m. p. h. A 420 h. p. engine is available in a more luxurious model. Comfortable! The roomy, 6-chair cabin can be fitted with office furnishings to suit the purchaser. Service! A countrywide network of Curtiss-Wright bases assured prompt service to Travel Air users wherever they fly.

Low Operating Cost: Actual figures, surprisingly low, on operating cost will be gladly furnished to interested executives and concerns. Full details of Travel Air construction and performance can be had by addressing Dept. T-**70**

TRAVEL AIR COMPANY
Division of CURTISS-WRIGHT
Sales Offices: 27 West 57th Street, New York

The Travel Air Cabin Monoplane of Black & Decker Mfg. Co. is regularly used by its air-minded officials. Here are Vice-President A. G. Decker and President S. D. Black setting out on one of their many time-saving flights with W. L. Snowden, Salesman-Pilot.

A PLANE FOR EVERY PURPOSE — *TRAVEL AIR*

The First Travel Air Built

Old Number One Comes Home to Stay

OLD Travel Air No. 1 has had an interesting career. Bought in 1924 by O. E. Scott, of St. Louis, its first trip was a call on Henry Ford. It was the first new production job Lindbergh ever flew. It has felt the hands of the great and near great at its controls. In it many prominent bankers, financiers and business men have flown. In it Nussinger and Ruth Elder have made more than one trip. And after having been all over the country on various missions it has at last come home to rest with the honor and sentiment that is its due.

This old ship has had 1750 hours in the air with no replacement. It is still airworthy—still trim. It doesn't look out of place among the latest Travel Air ships staked out along the line at the factory.

Following No. 1 have come hundreds of Travel Airs—in seven types—including the new Cabin Monoplane, "The Limousine of the Air"—each filling a commercial need—all characteristic of Travel Air proven performance with dependability.

The history of Travel Air has been a history of aggressiveness and progress from the day its first ship was built. Its ships are the standard of aircraft comparison and merit the full attention of dealers and prospective buyers the world over.

An interesting book telling the story of Travel Air is free on request

TRAVEL AIR
MANUFACTURING COMPANY
WICHITA, KANSAS

The Latest Type Travel Air

TRAVEL AIR
The Limousine of Air Travel

TYPE 6000

A De Luxe Monoplane combining Pullman Car comfort in air travel with proven performance and dependability.

CAPACITY—2 pilots, 4 passengers and 150 lbs. baggage, or pilot and 1000 lbs. pay load.

CONTROLS—Duel "dep" (side by side). Separate brake control pedals.

CABIN—All six occupants face forward with full front and side vision. Blue velour upholstering. Four removable wicker chairs. Windows, plate glass, raised and lowered by auto type crank lifts; heater; two full width doors.

LIGHTS—Instrument; navigation. Compartment arranged for landing lights.

POWER PLANT—200 H.P. Whirlwind J5C motor.

PERFORMANCE WITH NORMAL FULL LOAD. High speed; 126 mph. Landing speed, 57 mph. Normal cruising range (78 gal. fuel) 675-725 miles.

Complete specifications and details of equipment on request.

Travel Air Manufacturing Co.
Wichita, Kansas

IT has been a pleasure to present this story of Travel Air and a description of the current Travel Air models with the belief that it will not only be found interesting but conclusive proof of the enviable place this company holds in the field of aviation.

Despite a steadily increasing volume of business since the first Travel Air was built, the builders have resolutely avoided the temptation to sacrifice quality for quantity. This will always be the policy of Travel Air.

We feel it, therefore, but fair to suggest that orders be placed as far in advance of actual needs as possible. Special models, custom built and special equipment are furnished when desired, subject, however, to the necessary delay in their production. In every such instance the purchaser's wishes are paramount with us subject only to the demands of safe and recognized aeronautical practice.

Correspondence is invited. Prompt replies are assured. Any and all questions will be concisely and completely answered.

TRAVEL AIR COMPANY

©2013 Periscope Film LLC
All Rights Reserved
ISBN#978-1-937684-17-4
www.PeriscopeFilm.com

www.ingramcontent.com/pod-product-compliance
Lightning Source LLC
Chambersburg PA
CBHW081355040426
42451CB00017B/3465